ADVERSITY
FOR SALE

ADVERSITY FOR SALE

YOU GOTTA BELIEVE

■ ■ ■

JAY "JEEZY" JENKINS

WITH BENJAMIN MEADOWS-INGRAM

HarperCollins
LEADERSHIP

An Imprint of HarperCollins

Published by HarperCollins Leadership, an imprint of HarperCollins Focus LLC.

Any internet addresses, phone numbers, or company or product information printed in this book are offered as a resource and are not intended in any way to be or to imply an endorsement by HarperCollins Leadership, nor does HarperCollins Leadership vouch for the existence, content, or services of these sites, phone numbers, companies, or products beyond the life of this book.

ISBN 978-1-4002-3626-8 (eBook)
ISBN 978-1-4002-3625-1 (HC)

Library of Congress Control Number: 2023931455

Printed in the United States of America
23 24 25 26 27 LBC 8 7 6 5 4

CONTENTS

PART THREE

I used to hit the kitchen lights, cockroaches everywhere
Hit the kitchen lights, now it's marble floors everywhere
Call the carpenter, the roof on the coupe's gone
Give a fuck what he sold, I'm the truth, homes
Kitchen fumed up, niggas jamming Tupac
Get my Benihanas on, working two pots
Baby need shoes, partner need bail money
Bloodhound for the bread, I just smell money
You niggas just write, I recollect
Hands on, Jeezy really counted them checks
I'm Donald Trump in a white tee and white 1's
The conversation is money, nigga, you want some?

Aye . . . Aye . . .
Aye . . . Aye . . .
You gotta believe, you gotta believe
Aye . . .
You ain't never seen them pies
I'm talking so much white, it'll hurt ya eyes
I really lived it, man
Counted so much paper, it'll hurt ya hands

Let's get it!

—"THUG MOTIVATION 101"

(*Let's Get It: Thug Motivation 101*, 2005)

PREFACE

Now, check it. I'm not a mechanic, so this book isn't going to be about how to fix cars. And I'm not a plumber, so I can't tell you about how to fix pipes. And although I did work for a roofing company one summer—and we'll get to that—I'm not a roofer, so I can't really tell you anything about fixing roofs either. But I am a hustler. And I am a leader. And one thing I do know is how to get out there and get it. I've been doing it one way or another my whole life.

I can tell you straight up that coming from where I came from to making it to where I am today is just as significant as anything Bill Gates or any of those other multibillionaire CEOs you read about daily in the *Wall Street Journal* ever did, because I am a Black man in America who literally came from nothing. It wasn't just that I didn't have shit growing up; it's that no one around me and no one in my family ever had shit either. Everything I have today, I got it out of the mud with my bare hands with no gloves on.

The struggle was all I knew, but I had a bigger vision, and I think you should, too. One of my biggest goals was to be able to make money in my sleep, and not just because somebody was trapping for me at the other house down the block, but because the money I'd earned was working for me legally, aboveboard, through smart investments and strategic partnerships built on solid relationships that didn't come with all of the very real risks that come with doing business in the streets. And I wanted to show myself and the world that the skills I learned, while taking all the very real penitentiary chances I took, could translate to the corporate setting. To quote my guy DJ Drama, I think we accomplished that.

But it damn sure didn't come easy. Not at all.

Going legit isn't as simple as changing addresses or swapping out baggy sweats for a tailored Armani suit. You've got to have a crystal clear vision of who you are, where you want to be, and who you want to become. Not only that, but you're going to need a plan to get there and the discipline to execute that plan, no matter what it takes and regardless of any sacrifices you'll have to make. Because one thing's for certain, two things for sure—any goal worth reaching for is going to have some type of costs associated with it and breed all types of uncertainty along the way. And if it doesn't, then you've probably set your sights too low.

Most of all, you're going to have to have the right mindset because if you don't think you deserve the success you're after, or you don't think you have it in you to weather the storms, then you might as well give up now because you're destined to fail. Ain't no ifs, ands, or buts about it. But I don't care where you come from, what you've been through, or what you've done—if you can change your mindset, you can change your life.

I know because I've seen it firsthand, time and time again. And that's why I'm putting my life down on these pages, so you can hear how I did it, and hopefully it inspires you to go out and get it, too. That's not to say my goals are your goals, or that my path should be your path. Matter of fact, I hope you get where you're going without going through half the things I went through to get where I am today. But regardless of where you're at and where you're trying to go, I hope these words encourage you to continue chasing your dreams and to stay on your path, no matter what life throws your way.

Because things will happen, and people will try to talk down on your dreams and make you doubt yourself. You'll be amazed by how many times you'll hear that you can't do something from the people around you. They might not even realize they're doing it either because they won't come straight out and say, *Man, you can't do that*. It'll be more subtle things like, *That sounds expensive*, or, *That's really hard to do*, or, *No one gets two major label record deals before their debut*.

That's why I'm here to tell you: never listen to the naysayers, even if they mean well. Even the ones who tell you they love you. Even the ones in your own family. So get ya mind right. Take your dreams seriously, block out all the bullshit, and pursue your dreams with all you've got, because that's the only way you'll ever get where you're trying to go. And if you don't take anything else away from these pages, just know this one thing. It's the most important lesson I can ever share, and that's why it's the first thing I said on my Def Jam debut. The foundation to achieving any type of success—on the block or in the boardroom, in the streets or the corporate suites, in love, marriage, family, faith, life, health, or whatever—starts with one simple thing.

You gotta believe.

PART ONE

PART

ONE

Jumped Off the Porch

I can't even front, I started out as a thief.

At first it was little things, like stealing sodas out of the soda machine in front of this old mechanic's shop down the block from my grandmother's house. This was back in the 1980s and back then if your arm was skinny and long enough, you could push open the little trapdoor, reach up into the machine, and pull the cans loose. I used to run that little play all the time, at least until my arm got a little too big. I found that out the hard way, too. Reached up into the machine and next thing I knew I was stuck, and they had to call some adults to come down and help me get free.

I was embarrassed as hell about that, but I just know my grandmother felt a whole lot worse. She was my dad's mom—Mrs. Mattie Pickett—and she was a fixture in the community. At church every Sunday, worked at the local Head Start program, and ran numbers on the side. She'd had fifteen kids, including my dad, and even though she didn't have much, she was always taking in family. I stayed with her off and on through the years, and I wasn't the only one. There'd always be aunties and uncles and cousins and cousins' cousins coming in and out. If you ever needed some hot food and a place to stay, Mrs. Mattie Pickett was there. You might be sleeping six to a bed, but you'd have a bed. And you might not have much to eat, but you'd have some food.

Well, when she came and got me that day, she didn't pull me down the block by the ear the way you see old ladies do to little kids in the cartoons, but that's how it felt to me. I'll never forget that tight look on her face as she walked me home, either. Hot as hell but playing it cool in front of the neighbors, hissing at me under her breath like, "I can stand for a whole lot, but what I won't stand for are liars and thieves."

Needless to say, that was the last time I ran that little play, but that wasn't the only thing I took from that shop.

■ ■ ■

The shop was run by this old head, Mr. Russell. He was sort of like a mechanic-slash-salvage-man-slash-shopkeeper-slash-bank, and he was one of the first real entrepreneurs I ever met. He'd started with a backyard auto repair shop, expanded into the lot next door, and built himself a little real estate empire. Matter of fact, he was so well established on the north side of Hawkinsville, Georgia, that my grandmother's neighborhood was named after him. They called it Russell City.

For the most part, everybody in my family is from Hawkinsville. My grandmother, my dad, my mom, her mom, and all of my aunts and uncles and all that. And Hawkinsville is tiny. I'm talking 4,500 people on a good day, and even fewer back then. As you can imagine, there's not much to it. Couple of highways, some factories, a little small-town Main Street, some fast-food joints, a bunch of churches and liquor stores, and that's about it. But compared to all of the other little towns around there, Hawkinsville is big because it's the Pulaski County seat. Now, I'm not going to sit here and pretend like I know what all that entails, but for that little part of South Georgia, Hawkinsville is the hub. That's where the regional hospital is, the county schools, the courthouse, and the sheriff's offices. So if you live in any of those little surrounding towns and you've got some business to handle, you're coming to Hawkinsville to get it done.

As small as Hawkinsville is, though, it's big enough to have a 'hood. Put it this way: you might have to know what you're looking for to even find Hawkinsville on the map, but it does have a Martin Luther King Jr. Boulevard. It's just a short stretch of road on the north side of town, not too far from where my grandmother stayed, but remember when Chris Rock said, "I don't give a fuck where you are in America, if you're on a Martin Luther King Boulevard, there's some violence going down"?

Yeah, well, even in Hawkinsville that was true.

■ ■ ■

Old Mr. Russell had this car radio.

He had a lot of shit, really—old broken-down cars, refrigerators, TVs, and whatever else. And he'd just sit in his chair and watch you dig through it all until you found whatever it was you were looking for, and then he'd quote you a price.

But of all the stuff old Mr. Russell had, what I really wanted was that car radio.

This was the late eighties, and the flyest thing you could have in your car back then was an Alpine two-knob pullout tape deck. Old Mr. Russell's wasn't an Alpine, but it was that style and that was good enough for me. And I knew if I was smart and I played it right, I just might be able to get it for free.

At the time, old Mr. Russell was sort of trying to look out for me. I was only about eleven or twelve years old, but I'd already developed a rep as a troublemaker. And because he and my grandmother were close, at a certain point she asked him to take me under his wing. I guess the way they were looking at it, the more time I spent at old Mr. Russell's shop, the less time I had to get into trouble in the streets.

I'd started going over to old Mr. Russell's spot pretty much every day after school, helping him out here and there, and then whenever what had to be done was done, I'd pull up a chair next to his and keep an eye on the shop while he slept. That's when the trouble started to brew. Hours and hours would go by, days sometimes, with nobody stopping by, and I'd just sit there with my eyes on the prize.

He kept the radio on a shelf high on the wall, next to a bunch of other junk collecting dust. The way I was looking at it, he must not have cared about it all that much—otherwise he would have kept it somewhere else to protect it and keep it safe. But that radio was everything to me. So I made a plan.

For the next few days, whenever I'd go over there, I'd wait for him to fall asleep and then I'd move my chair closer and closer to the shelf. I took my time with it so it didn't seem like suddenly one day my chair was in a whole other place. Then, when I finally felt like I'd gotten close enough, I watched his eyes to see if he could see me. I'd make my move when I was sure he was asleep.

I made sure to wear a baggy black shirt that day. Then, just like always, I stopped by his spot after school to see if he needed any help. Just like always, I straightened a few things up here and there, and then we settled into our chairs and I waited for him to fall asleep.

In the end, it wasn't all that deep. When the time came, I stood up on my chair, grabbed the radio, stuffed it under my shirt, and walked right out the door. I doubt old Mr. Russell even cracked an eye.

When I got back to my grandmother's house, I went straight to the room I was staying in, cleared some space on the dresser, and pulled the radio out from under my shirt. I didn't care that it wasn't an Alpine. It looked great, and I felt like I'd really pulled something off.

I'd made a plan, executed that plan, and I hadn't gotten caught. That was big to me. And then, after a few weeks of messing with it and trying to get it to work, that knockoff Alpine wasn't enough. I wanted the real deal. Even more than that, though, in my grandmother's tiny-ass house in that tiny-ass town without a dollar to my name, I really just wanted more.

■ ■ ■

I never went back to Mr. Russell's shop after that. I don't know if he ever noticed the radio was missing or if he even cared. I never heard anything about it if he did.

What's crazy is that when I look back on that incident, I bet old Mr. Russell probably would have just given me that radio if I'd asked. Real shit. And that's a real lesson, too—before you take something from someone, just ask, because they just might give it to you and you'll maintain the relationship. But once you take something from someone, that's it. Even if you eventually come clean and give it back, the damage to the relationship is done, and you'll both have to live with that.

Of course, I wasn't thinking like that back then. Mr. Russell had something I wanted, so I took it. I cared more about the radio than the relationship. And the crazy thing is, I was still so young it would be years before I even had a car.

■ ■ ■

I don't remember the day we landed at Naha Airport, but I know for a fact I wasn't in a good mood. I never liked leaving Georgia. I had family in the 'Ville. I had friends. I knew the culture and the people, who to fuck with and who to avoid. And even when I was getting in trouble, I felt safe, almost like, "What's the worst that can happen to me here?" Even the sheriff seemed cool to me. Not cool like *cool*, but cool like he had a good relationship with my grandmother, and we were all on a first-name basis so I couldn't imagine him ever locking me up no matter what I did. I guess what I'm saying is, Hawkinsville was home.

Okinawa on the other hand? Shit, Okinawa was Japan. And coming straight out of South Georgia, I definitely didn't know a damn thing about that.

My dad was in the Marines, and we were always moving when I was young. That's how I ended up being born in Columbia, South Carolina, even though the rest of my family was from the 'Ville. But no matter where we were—Fort Gordon in Augusta, Camp Lejeune in North Carolina, or K-Bay in Hawaii—I always gravitated toward the bad kids because that's what I knew.

Looking back, I can see how all my acting out was really rooted in some combination of me trying to get attention, trying to get things to make myself feel better about a fucked-up situation, and just trying to survive. In the 'hood, I didn't feel out of place. Everybody was going through something and dysfunctional families were the norm. Shit, in the 'hood, being bad was almost a good thing, because it was a way to fit in.

But the base wasn't the 'hood, and every time we'd show up somewhere new, I always felt out of place. It was one thing when we were still in the South and the 'hood was just a few hours away. But Hawaii? Japan? C'mon. I'm Black, I'm country, I've got a 'hood mentality, and I'm on the other side of the world and way behind all the other kids in school. They're rushing home for dinner at six o'clock sharp, doing chores, and pursuing interests like violin and flute, when I know about things like shoplifting, and the movies with the cussing in them, and how to get with girls. I was one of the kids the other parents warned their kids about. And I definitely didn't know a damn thing about no flute!

I always felt like the odd man out, so I'd fall back on what I excelled at, and then I'd go looking for my tribe. It never took me long to find it either. No matter where we were in the world, give me a couple of days on a new base and I'd be running with the few other kids out there who were stealing money out of their momma's purse, taking liquor from their dad's stash, getting into fights, smoking cigarettes, and paying more attention to playing ball and getting girls than anything going on in school. And one way or another, wherever we went, I always ended up being the leader of the pack.

■ ■ ■

In Okinawa, I made the whole island my playground. And I ran wild.

The first little scheme I cooked up was at the Exchange. Now, if you don't know anything about military life, the Exchange is basically the base's mall. That's where you go to get all the things you might want from back home—clothes, furniture, electronics and TVs, music, movies, and all that. Once we got settled in, one of the first things I noticed was that the security at the Camp Butler Exchange was really, really lax. So I went to work.

The first thing I stole was the Geto Boys' *Grip It! On That Other Level*. This was back when you could still get all the new music on cassette, so I just slipped the tape in my pocket and walked right out the door. I ran that play a couple of times, and then I decided to level up.

Back then, if you really wanted to get fresh, it was all about the Cross Colours with the Hi-Tec "Jodeci" boots. That was the look. Of course my family couldn't afford all that, so one day I hit the

Exchange with an old shopping bag tucked under my shirt and an old receipt. I took the bag into the dressing room, put all the clothes I wanted in it, threw that old receipt on top, and walked right out the door. I ran that play so many times while we were there that I was voted Best Dressed in school—and I never spent a dime.

But it was during my solo missions off base that I really did my thing. I used to bike all over the island, checking out the culture and taking it all in. It was so different from home: the food, the way people dressed, the cars, the language. Every once in a while, I'd come across these young guys in their early twenties, and they were always driving these old-school Cadillacs, with their hair slicked back and their arms all tatted up. They seemed so cool to me. One of my homies over there was this cat, Ko. He was half-Black and half-Japanese and when I asked him about them, he told me all about the Yakuza, which is like the Japanese mob.

Ko put me onto a lot of things, and his mom was the one who really opened my mind to Japanese cuisine. I used to go over to his place all the time, and she'd bring out all these sushi rolls and rice balls and teach me about everything she was serving. Of course, back in the 'hood no one knew anything about eating raw fish, but there I was on the other side of the world, soaking up game.

Still, somebody should have warned the Japanese about me. Coming from where I'm from, you can't leave your clothes out drying on the line without worrying that somebody might come by and snatch them up. But Japanese culture is all about honor and integrity, so the level of trust is through the roof. In the States, especially as a young Black male, you walk in a store and it feels like all eyes are on you. But when I was in Japan, sometimes I'd walk into a shop and it'd feel like no one was even watching the store, much less me.

So it didn't take long before I found this one electronics shop and . . .

Got 'em.

A brand-new sleek and slim Sony Walkman that looked like it was twenty years ahead of the big chunky ones you could get back home. Fit right in my pocket, too, so I walked straight out that door, hopped on my bike, and cruised right on back to the base with no problems at all.

A few months later, we were back in the 'Ville visiting family while my dad was on leave, and one of my older cousins noticed the headphones hanging around my neck.

"Yo, lemme see those!"

I handed over my Walkman and as soon as he saw it, he was like, "Goddamn, Lil' J! Where'd you get that?"

I told him about the electronics shops in Japan and how everything over there was some space-age, futuristic shit.

He turned it over in his hands, studying it. "You think you can get some walkie-talkies like this?"

"Yeah," I told him. "How much you got?"

He laughed. "How 'bout you get 'em first and then we can figure out the price?"

Shit. Say less, right?

The next time I took my bike off base, I rolled around looking for another electronics shop and then . . .

Got 'em again.

But instead of going right back to the base, I just kept going. Next shop, same play. Next shop, same play. And on and on, until finally when I got back to the base, I had maybe five or six sets. I packed everything up, slapped a Georgia address on it, and sent it out.

A few weeks later, my cousin called. And he was hype.

"Yo, these walkie-talkies are the shit! Can you get some more?"

I laughed. "You're feeling them, huh?"

He was like, "Man, what? I'll take as many as you can get!"

When I asked him about the price, he said, "Shit, it's whatever. You tell me. Just keep 'em coming and we'll figure it out."

For the next year or so, that's what I did. In the end, I probably made a few Gs off that little scheme all in. And it wasn't just Walkmen and walkie-talkies either. It was whatever I could get my hands on. You could say that was my first business. I was a Japanese electronics importer/exporter, and everything I carried, I stole.

I never did get caught off base, but at a certain point the guards at the Exchange finally smartened up and grabbed me one time when I was trying to walk out the door. I'll tell you what, the military doesn't play when it comes to thieves and for a minute there, it looked like they might even try to court-martial my dad.

After that, my dad sent my mom, my little sister, and me back home. They weren't happy about that—but it was fine by me. I'd felt so out of place, I couldn't wait to get back to the 'hood.

CHAPTER TWO

Loyalty Ain't a Word, It's a Lifestyle

My older cousins were legends in my family. They lived in a big house on a nice plot of land in Decatur, just outside of East Atlanta. My cousin Cuzzo bought that house for my auntie and it was beautiful, tall, and tucked way back in a nice neighborhood with a long driveway. My dad would take my sister and me up to see them sometimes, and at the time it was the biggest house I'd ever seen.

Cuzzo was the oldest, and he was a pretty boy. Real smooth with the ladies and he knew how to dress. He was always on trend. Black was a little younger, and he was really into music. Really, they both were, but whereas Cuzzo was more interested in the business side, Black studied the art. He was a music head and a DJ, too, so he was always up on the latest artists and songs. He had his DJ setup in the garage and whenever we'd go up to see them, I'd always sit out there and watch him practice mixing. Everything about it was dope to me, and I loved watching him do his thing.

And then one day, when I was still young, he let me get on. We'd been out in that garage all day when he started powering down, like, "That's it, bro. I'm out."

He must have seen the look on my face as he was about to hit the lights because I didn't even have to ask.

"You want to mess around a little bit while I'm gone?"

Man, what? Listen, he didn't have to ask me twice.

Black laughed and turned everything back on. "Just don't scratch my shit," he said, and then he was gone.

You want to talk about being in a happy place? I was in heaven. This wasn't some broken-down, knockoff Alpine I'd swiped from old Mr. Russell's shop. This was a real deal, top-of-the-line DJ setup, with crates full of the hottest records out on deck. You already know I stayed in that garage all night mixing J.J. Fad's "Supersonic" into Salt-N-Pepa's "Push It" into Afrika Bambaataa and the Soulsonic Force's "Planet Rock," or trying to anyway, and on and on and on. Of course, I didn't really know what I was doing at first, but I was determined to learn. Whenever we went to Decatur after that, I'd head straight to the garage and if my cousin didn't have those turntables tied up, I'd jump on and get to work, and practice, practice, practice.

There was another reason I loved being in that garage, though: the cars. My cousins stayed in new whips. I'm talking the Eddie Bauer Explorers with the leather interior, the crazy-ass Nissan 300ZXs, all that. I saw every single one of them in my cousins' garage first, and everything was always rimmed up and tricked out. They'd drop ten to fifteen grand on top of whatever they'd paid for the car just to make sure their shit was extra tight.

I'm telling you, my cousins were fresh as hell. They were a part of that first generation running around Atlanta with that dope-boy swag, doing it up and giving cats like Deion Sanders and Dominique Wilkins a run for their money in the clubs, which makes perfect sense because that's exactly what they were: straight-up dope boys. And in the early 1990s, my cousins were getting paid.

■ ■ ■

I always like to say I'm third-generation Third Coast, meaning I'm just the third generation of my family that wasn't born into American slavery. And instead of moving up to the other big northern cities during the Great Migration, my family stayed right where they were, in the deep Deep South.

My family is from the heart of the Black Belt, the cradle of cotton production. For two hundred years, my people—*our* people— literally slaved away on plantations just down the road from the 'Ville, growing and harvesting the crop that helped transform some rebellious-ass British colonies into a global empire. But before me, there was no generational wealth in my family. There was no rich auntie or uncle waiting in the wings to swoop in and help cover the bills or pay for college when the time came. Nobody had a connection at the admissions office or a lead on an internship to help us on our way. All we had was each other and the 'hood. And even though the 'hood I came up in was literally built right on top of the very same land that my people worked to make this country filthy rich, all my people—*our* people—ever had to show for it was generational trauma and widespread, persistent poverty and pain.

And then when crack came along, it was like pouring gasoline on the whole shit.

WHOOSH!

Crack set the 'hood on fire and it hasn't been the same since.

■ ■ ■

I don't think I'd be where I am today if it wasn't for the basketball courts. They were right across the street from my grandmother's house and even though there wasn't much to them, they were our Rucker Park.

Every Sunday, all the best ballplayers from all over the county would come through to hoop, and the whole 'hood would come out to watch. It was like the main event. And whenever my cousins were in town, they'd pull up on those courts like Magic and Kareem in their prime. And not because they were really hooping like that either, but because of how they were balling in the streets. They'd hop out of whatever they were riding in, rims gleaming, jewels shining, clothes fresh as hell, finger waves in their hair, some fine-ass thing on their arm, and their pockets on swole. *Showtime.*

I was born in 1977 so I was just a kid when the crack era really popped off. I remember being eight, nine years old and walking to school and seeing the little empty baggies on the ground or hearing *so-and-so's mom is a crackhead* and things like that, but I was too young to understand what was really going on. I didn't know anything about drug use or addiction and the toll those things can take on a community. All I knew was that my cousins were getting money, and it was like Christmas whenever they came to town.

We could eat the food we wanted to eat, all the kids had money for ice cream and Gatorade, and we'd have a big family cookout in my grandmother's front yard. Everybody would be happy, and it was always a good vibe. And then they'd leave and all that good energy would be gone.

So whenever my cousins were in town, I'd be posted up at that park watching them do their thing. And they weren't the only hustlers out there, either. There were other cats that would come through from other cities and towns, and they'd all link up with my cousins and some of the local guys and do what they had to do.

Things would get live on the court, but I was always way more interested in the plays my cousins and them were running on the sidelines, and I spent a whole lot of Sundays back then in my front-row seats, trying to soak up their game. And one of the first lessons I learned was one of the most valuable lessons of all: *Stay loyal and keep your motherfucking mouth shut.*

■ ■ ■

Remember when I said, *Bloodhound for the bread, I just smell money* on "Thug Motivation 101"? Yeah, well, that's real. Ever since I was a kid, I've had a sixth sense when it comes to cash. I'll admit, that's another reason why I always loved going up to my cousins' house in Decatur: the bread.

It helped that my cousins kept any cash they had lying around the crib in a couple of regular spots, so once I found those, I'd wait until the coast was clear and take my little taste. I'd get a grand here, or a grand there. It was a lot of money to me at the time, but it wasn't shit to them. Put it this way: when you're skimming a rack or two from a half million dollars stuffed in the sofa, nobody ever knows.

After a while, I started to think I was slick. And then I got caught.

It was the summer between fifth and sixth grade, and I'd been staying with them for weeks. But summer was over, and it was time to go back to the 'hood.

Their sister had just had a baby, and she'd set up the nursery upstairs right next to her room. I'd been scoping the house the whole trip, but all the regular stash spots were bare. Maybe they'd finally noticed they'd been coming up a little short. Either way, I decided to make one last sweep. And that's when I found the bag.

It was in the crib, peeking out from under the blanket. When I saw it, I was like, *Oh, shit!* And then I did something that I still don't understand to this day. Instead of taking my normal little piece, I took the whole bag. There I was, twelve years old, can't drive, and hours away from home. That was one of those rare instances when I definitely *didn't* have a plan.

I took the bag downstairs and stuffed it under the couch, and then I sat down to wait for my aunt to finish up whatever she was doing and take me home. Waiting for her was like watching the clock at school.

Tick . . . tick . . . tick . . .

When Cuzzo noticed the bag was missing, I heard him holler at his brother in the garage, like, "Yo! What happened to that bag in the crib?"

Black cut the music, and from my seat on the couch, I heard Cuzzo ask him again.

"Shit, I put it in there," Black said, walking into the kitchen.

Cuzzo was like, "Well, it's not in there now." I could tell he was getting hot, but Black didn't seem all that concerned.

"Maybe sis moved it," he said.

"Man, why the fuck would she do that?"

"I don't know, shit," Black said. "Maybe 'cause it was in the way of the baby?"

"Well, where'd she put it then?"

Black was like, "Fuck if I know, do I look like her?"

"Nah, you look like the dumb motherfucker that just lost a bag."

Black didn't appreciate that and they started really going at it. Meanwhile, I was sitting on the couch keeping my mouth shut. The way I was looking at it, if I made it out of there with the bag, that was on them. But that was one big *if.*

Then Black was like, "Yo, matter of fact, my beeper was in that bag. Call my beeper."

My ears shot up. Cuzzo picked up the kitchen phone, and sure enough . . .

Beep-beep—beep-beep—beep-beep!

Right under my ass.

Man, those motherfuckers almost killed me over that shit, I swear. Looking back, I really don't know how I made it back to the 'hood in one piece, but I guess I was still so young that they decided to give me a pass. It was the only one I'd need.

■ ■ ■

As much time as I spent up in Atlanta with them, my cousins spent way more time down in Hawkinsville with us. I really couldn't understand it at the time. Why would you want to kick it in the country when you had the whole city at your feet? When I got older and got in the game myself, I understood.

The big city has its perks, but there's lots of money to be made in the small towns. In Atlanta, they were fighting over the same turf as everyone else, but they were running things in the 'Ville. Not only that, but because Hawkinsville functions almost like a hub for all those other small towns, my cousins could come down with all their work, post up at my auntie's house, and do their thing. Less competition + less stress + more bread = easy money. That's Business 101. When you control the market, you control the price, and that's when you rake in the dough.

So that's another lesson I learned from them. But that one came later, after I was way more advanced. That first one, though—stay loyal and keep your motherfucking mouth shut? That one still needed to sink in.

■ ■ ■

So Black was dating this chick, right? Let's call her Angela. And Angela was the shit. Super cool and fine as hell. I think she saw me like a little brother because we had that kind of rapport.

This was right around the time of the whole beeper incident, but summer was over and I was back in the 'hood. My cousins were dipping in and out of the 'Ville, doing their thing, and Black started messing with this girl who stayed around the way.

Well, one day I was over at those basketball courts when Angela walked up like, "Hey, Lil' J, you know when Black's gon' be back in town?"

Because I was young and naive, I didn't think twice before telling her the truth, like, "Shit, he's been here. He was at Granny's house with one of his girls just the other day."

"Oh, yeah?" she said. "What's the girl's name?"

And that's how she played me.

The next time I saw Black, he was busting through my grandmother's front door, like, "Lil' J! Where the fuck you at?"

I lit out the back and just kept running. I didn't know what he wanted but I could tell by the tone in his voice that I didn't want to know. He chased me all over the 'hood until I finally looked over my shoulder and saw he wasn't there. I bent over to catch my breath, and that's when a couple of my friends walked up talking about, "Man, what's going on? What did you do?" and all that.

Then one of my other little partners came up like, "Yo, you know your cousin's around the corner mixing up a big bowl full of dog shit."

I was like, "Dog shit? Man, what the fuck for?"

Next thing I know, Black came tearing around the corner with a big-ass bowl in his hands. Everybody took off running. My friends thought it was funny, but I knew Black wasn't playing. He starts chasing me through the streets again, but this time Black wasn't about to lose.

It was all eyes on us, when . . . *BAM!* He grabbed me and dumped that whole bowl of dog shit, right on my head.

Right when I was gagging off the smell, he hit me with a roundhouse kick right to the chest that knocked me straight into a tree. I don't know how that motherfucker knew karate, but he damn sure got me with that one. Knocked the breath right out of me, too. Then he jumped on top of me and just started whaling.

Blow after blow, he was like, "Motherfucker! Don't you ever tell on me! And don't you ever tell on your family!"

I was crouched in a ball, pleading my case. "I was just telling her where you was!"

"No! This how shit go!" He kept hitting me. *Bam. Bam. Bam.* "You don't tell! You don't steal! And you damn sure better respect me!"

"Okay! Okay! Okay!" I screamed.

When he finally stopped, I looked up and saw him standing over me.

"And don't you ever forget it neither," he said. And then he walked away.

I slowly picked myself up and limped back to my grandmother's house. I smelled like shit and my whole body hurt like hell. Even worse, everybody in the 'hood had seen the whole thing.

When my grandmother saw me coming up her drive, she stepped outside and waved me in, like, "Come on in here, baby. It's going to be all right."

"Granny, he embarrassed me in front of all my friends!" I sobbed.

But she knew the stakes. My cousins were always helping her out, paying bills and giving her a little extra cash, and she wasn't the only one in the family they were helping like that either. For the most part, everybody knew what was up.

"You can't be telling people about what they're doing, okay, baby?" she said, as she helped me get cleaned up. "Their business is their business, just like yours is yours. It's no one else's concern."

And that's how I learned that. *Stay loyal and keep your mother-fucking mouth shut.*

CHAPTER THREE

Let's Get It

I've never been scared of hard work. If the money's out there and the only thing that's stopping me from getting it is putting in the work, you might as well go on and pay me now because I assure you, that work will get done.

We can't change where we're from, who our families are, or what kind of resources we have at the start, but we can control how hard we work. There's always more we can do to reach that extra gear: another hour to put in, more research to do, or another take to try to get it right. I'm not saying the Gospel of Hard Work is the be-all and end-all of success, but it's a cornerstone of it—that's for damn sure.

We all have choices to make when it comes to how we use our time and how we go about pursuing our dreams. We can talk about it, or we can be about it. That's not to say all of your dreams will come true if you simply put in the work—they may or they may not—but I guarantee you if you don't put in the work, that's all they'll ever be: dreams.

■ ■ ■

When I was thirteen, I went to work for my uncle throwing watermelons. He wasn't one of my blood uncles—more of a family friend, but you know how that goes in the 'hood.

He had a roadside watermelon stand, and every day he'd swing by my grandmother's and scoop me up at the crack of dawn, and then we'd ride out to his field and I'd spend the whole morning throwing watermelons, loading up his truck with the rest of his crew. Then we'd ride back to town and spend the rest of the day hustling watermelons by the side of the road.

It paid about fifty dollars a week, which was good money for me at the time, and at the end of the week, I'd take all the money I'd made and get him to change it all out so I could have a twenty, two fives, and twenty ones. Then, I'd put the twenty-dollar bill on top and fold it into a little bankroll.

Walking around the 'hood with that little knot in my pocket, I thought I was so fresh. And I also liked knowing that I'd earned my money the right way. Throwing watermelons wasn't some shit I pulled just to get some quick bread. It was slow, hard work that I could feel all in my back, arms, and legs, and I knew I was getting stronger physically, mentally, and financially just by showing up and doing the work. For the first time in my life, I felt like I was making real, steady progress toward my goals. I felt like I was growing up.

Still, fifty dollars a week is just fifty dollars a week, no matter how you fold your bills, and I knew throwing watermelons was only going to get me so far. I was going to have to find something else if I ever wanted to get where I was really trying to go.

■ ■ ■

After spending the summer throwing watermelons, I spent that fall working on roofs. Well, sort of. Another one of my neighborhood uncles had a roofing company and I was the little kid running around the job site with a wheelbarrow doing all of the things that nobody else wanted to do—clean up *this*, move *that*, and all that.

Throwing watermelons was hard work but working for the roofing company was more of a job. Everybody had their own responsibilities, and my uncle was like a drill sergeant keeping everybody in line. He was a hard-ass and I didn't like the way he talked to me sometimes because he was always talking shit, but he was the first real boss I'd ever been around and I admired how he ran his crew. If we had ten days to finish a job, we were done in nine and onto the next. I never saw him arguing with a client or having any kind of issues when it came to things like that. His people were organized, efficient, and effective. He rode us like a motherfucker but at the end of the day, he got the job done, he paid his employees on time, and he had a successful business that he owned.

I made twenty dollars a day working for him, and every time I watched him count everybody out from a big stack of cash at the end of the week and put that $100 in my hand, I'd think, *When I grow up, I want to be like* that.

■ ■ ■

In the 'Ville, working a factory job was the big thing. It's consistent work with good benefits and decent pay so you're winning if you've got one of those. Coming up, I knew a bunch of people who worked a factory job their whole lives, and that was nothing to be ashamed of either, because for the most part everybody I knew who didn't have a factory job was bottom-of-the-barrel broke. I'm talking *broke* broke.

Just to put some numbers on it, according to the 1990 US census, when I was thirteen, over half of the Black population in the 'Ville was living below the poverty line with a median household income of less than $13,000 a year. According to that same census, a third of Hawkinsville's Black population didn't even have a phone.

I knew a couple of people whose parents had decent jobs, but they were few and far between. From what I could tell, it seemed like everybody else just hung out at the liquor store all day and collected a government check. And absolutely none of that appealed to me.

I wasn't interested in working for somebody else or collecting a government check or doing just enough to get by. I wanted to be my own boss, build businesses, make deals, and get into situations where I could make money in my sleep. Most of all, I wanted to be free.

Over the years, I've gotten to know a lot of people who are perfectly happy living that all-American, middle-class life. My dad's brother Hoss and his family are like that, and they're honestly some of the happiest people I've ever known. But my ambition was always to be greater than that. And realizing my vision meant I needed more.

Real talk and no bullshit, even at a young age, I saw myself running an empire.

■ ■ ■

As the days got shorter and the months dragged on, my pockets dried up. When it came to getting money, the winter of 1991–92 was the first time I'd experienced a drought.

I remember sitting in class at Pulaski Middle School, watching the minutes tick off the clock and feeling like I was wasting so much time. After spending the summer at my grandmother's house, I was back to staying with my mom and my sister in a two-bedroom trailer that my mom was leasing to own on the outskirts of town.

That thing was so small, there was barely any room to think. I swear, you could stand in the middle of it, reach out, and just about touch the walls.

My mom was really going through it. My dad was off seeing the world on the military's dime and she was back in the 'hood with three mouths to feed. She'd gotten a job as a housekeeper on the other side of town, but it didn't really pay for shit and every day she'd come home exhausted and mad. I didn't know the details of whatever was going on between her and my dad. All I knew was that he was gone, we were broke, and when my mom would get to drinking it felt like she'd try to take all of her anger out on me.

She'd call me all types of names and tell me I wasn't good for shit. The truth is, I'd been hearing it all my life. One of my aunts even used to call me Jerry's Kids because she thought I was slow. And she wasn't the only one. It seemed like everybody was always telling me I wouldn't amount to shit.

That's one of the reasons I'd been so proud to have those jobs. I'd get paid and come home and show my mom the cash, like, "Look what I made!" I knew it wasn't much in the scheme of things, but in that town a couple hundred dollars was a lot, especially for a kid. And being able to point to the cash in hand was almost like a way of showing the whole world my worth. Including myself.

Looking back, I can appreciate my mom's tough love because it helped make me strong. But whenever things would get real bad between us, I'd go back to my grandmother's house to escape. That was the only place I ever felt unconditional love. It didn't matter what kind of trouble I'd gotten into, how bad I was doing in school, how much money I had in my pocket, or whatever else was going on in my life, good, bad, or ugly—Mrs. Mattie Pickett was there, and her house always felt like home.

■ ■ ■

One of those nights when I was over there trying to get some space from my mom and maybe a little something to eat, I was sitting in the kitchen and feeling about as worthless as a wooden frying pan when my uncle Bo Slick walked in.

"That ain't the end of the chicken, is it?" he said.

I told him there were a couple of pieces left.

"Good," he said, sitting down. "So I won't have to fight you for it, then. Save you the embarrassment."

Bo Slick is one of my dad's brothers, and he was the funniest motherfucker. He always had jokes. Matter of fact, he's the one who gave my second cousin the nickname Gold Mouth. His real name was Dawaun, but he had this one gold tooth with his initial on it—"D"—and every time he'd come around, my uncle Bo Slick would be like, "Oh, shit, here comes ol' Gold Mouth!" And it stuck.

Bo Slick had been on disability ever since some guys caught him coming down the path to my grandmother's house late one night and beat him damn near half to death trying to rob him. He walked with a cane and a big ol' arch in his back, and he spent most of his time drinking, cracking jokes, and talking shit.

"What the hell's the matter with you? Sittin' in here looking like a wet cat," he said, looking me over. When I didn't say anything, he was like, "Man, you might be too sad to eat that hot chicken. How 'bout I have that and you get to whatever's left in the fridge?"

The microwave dinged, but I didn't move.

"Goddamn, Lil' J. What is it?"

I started to say something like, "Man, I just . . ." But I broke off.

We sat there in silence for a minute, and then he was like, "Shit, if you don't start talking, I'ma start eating, so which is it?"

He made like he was about to grab his cane. Fucking Bo Slick, man. Always talking shit.

I can't front, though: that night it worked. While we sat there eating in my grandmother's kitchen, I opened up and told him about everything that was going on with me. How my mom was on my ass. How my dad had left us in that trailer to go off to wherever he was. How every day at school I felt like I was wasting my time. How I had bigger dreams than just getting a factory job, and how I felt like instead of getting closer to realizing those dreams, I was going in reverse.

"Well, you know I know life ain't no motherfuckin' cakewalk," he said when I was done, tapping the top of his cane. "But you know I'll do anything for you that I can."

"'Preciate that, Unc."

"Yeah, well," he said, trailing off. "What do you think is the worst part of it all?"

I thought about it for a second. To be honest, at that exact moment everything felt bad. But if I had to boil it down to one thing?

"I guess it's that I don't have any money," I told him.

Bo Slick looked at me. I can't imagine what he thought. Me, fourteen years old, sitting in my grandmother's kitchen, stressing.

"Well, I don't have much, but if you think it'll help, I can give you this," he said.

He pulled a crumpled-up $20 bill out of his pocket and set it on the table between us.

I was like, "Aw, man, Unc." I knew what $20 meant in that house. Shit, I knew what $20 meant in that whole town.

"Well, you want it or not? 'Cause if you don't, I'll just . . ." He made like he was about to take it back.

"Nah, nah, I'll take it." I reached for the bill. "It's just . . . are you sure?"

"Yeah, shit, it's just money," he said. "If you think you can do something with it that'll help you get out of whatever this mood is, take it. It's yours. I'll get some more some kind of way."

He stood up to clear his plate. I picked the $20 off the table and smoothed it out. I couldn't believe he'd give me the last $20 from his disability check just like that.

"You sure?" I asked him again.

He was like, "Boy, I'ma start charging you $20 every time you ask me a stupid question, so you better not ask me again."

When he was gone, I looked at that wrinkled-ass $20 bill in my hand.

This is what I'm worth right now, I thought.

Then, I started thinking about all the things that I could do with it. I can't front, the first thing that came to mind was junk food. Like, *Maybe I'll go down to the corner store and get some chips, a soda, some little Hostess cupcakes*—all those things felt like luxuries to me.

Then I thought, *Maybe I'll hold off for now and take this $20 and put it toward something bigger, like some new clothes or a pair of the new Nike Andre Agassis and get back to my Best Dressed ways.*

Or maybe I could do something else with it. Something productive. Something I'd never done before. Maybe I could take that $20, put it to work, and slowly but surely, start building my empire.

Sitting at that kitchen table looking at that bill, in that tiny-ass house in that little-ass town in the middle of South Georgia surrounded by a whole lot of nothing, I told myself, *You know what? I'm going to take this $20 and I'm never going to ask anyone for any handouts ever again.*

■ ■ ■

At the time, Gold Mouth had been messing with this chick down in Pineview, which was this other little town not too far from the 'hood. She had a couple of sisters, and they were all bad. They were kind of like the Kardashians of Pineview. Everybody wanted to get with them, and some kind of way, Gold Mouth had made it happen with one of them so we were always going down there to kick it with her.

Well, one of her sisters was seeing this cat who was hustling. He wasn't big-time or anything, but he was in the game and that night, I decided to go down to Pineview to see him. I was still too young to drive legally, but my grandmother would let me borrow her car sometimes to run around town.

It's about a twenty-minute drive from Hawkinsville to Pineview, and my mind was racing the whole time, running through everything I planned to do, like, *I'm going to get there and see ol' girl, then I'm going to get her to take me to see her man, then I'm going to see if he can link me with his man, then I'm going to come back to the 'hood, and . . .*

In Pineview, everything went according to plan. Ol' girl took me to see her man and her man took me to see his guy. His guy lived in a trailer on the outside of town, and he was one of the main guys in the area. He had a Florida plug, and one thing about Florida back then, Florida had that butter. I'm talking golden brown, not too white and not too hard. That's what you wanted. You wanted that butter.

He was also selling double-ups, which meant if you spent $20 with him, what you got back was worth $40 on the street if you worked it right. So I spent $20 with him, and about a half hour later, I was headed back up to the 'Ville in my grandmother's old gray Oldsmobile with a $20 sack of butter in my pocket worth $40 on the street, and my mind racing with nothing but high hopes.

This $20 will get me $40 and that $40 will get me $80 and . . .

When I got back to the 'hood, I bought the cheapest pack of razor blades I could find at the corner store, then walked a few blocks over to my Auntie Mother's house. Her real name was Brent, but everybody in the family called her Mother. You know how I say, *Hide the rest of the yams at my auntie house* on "And Then What?" That's her.

There was a little party going on at Auntie Mother's when I got there, but that was a regular thing. There was always something going on over there. People playing cards, gambling, drinking, talking shit. Her place was almost like the underground neighborhood club, which ended up being great for me, but that was later on.

I ducked into my cousin Paul's room to get some privacy and shut the door. I took the sack out of my pocket and looked at it. It was nothing but one of those old fold-over sandwich bags, but inside there was this one golden brown nugget.

Goddamn, I thought, looking at it. *That looks like freedom.*

I'd never messed with crack before, but I knew enough about it to know what to do next. I split that butter right down the middle, tore the sandwich bag in half, put one rock in one corner, the other in the other, scraped the shake off the table, and tied them off.

And then I hit the block.

■ ■ ■

In Hawkinsville, everybody hustled on Poplar Street. That was the trap.

Now, just to get a couple definitions out the way real quick: *The trap* is anywhere you're comfortable getting money. I've seen guys trap out of their cars, abandoned houses, mansions, and anything and everything in between. *Trappin'* is working the trap or hustling generally, really. And *trap music* is the soundtrack to all of it. Of course, back when I first hit the block, trap music didn't exist, mainly because we hadn't created it yet. That's another one of those things that happened later on.

Poplar Street was a short little overgrown dog-legged stretch of road not too far from MLK, with some low-income apartments on one side and a bunch of abandoned shotgun homes on the other. It wasn't too far from Auntie Mother's house so that night I walked over and posted up with nothing but those two rocks in my pocket, my ambition, and a dream.

It was already late, but Poplar Street was poppin'. The hustlers were out doing their thing, the cars were coming through with customers being served. I'd never been out there before so it took me a minute to catch my first sale, but when I did, I took all the bills the guy gave me—a ten, a five, and five ones—lined them all up, folded them in half, and put the ten on the outside. I'd hustled up my first little bankroll, and I had one thought as I stuffed it in my front pocket: *Hell yeah.*

The second sale took even longer than the first, and I ended up being out there so long that when the guy told me he didn't have the full $20, I just sold him what I had for $18. Still, walking back to my grandmother's house with $38 in my pocket, I felt like I'd cracked a safe. There wasn't a whole lot of money in it at the moment, but now I had the code. And I knew that if I just kept coming back, eventually it would pay off.

I was on my way.

■ ■ ■

After that first night, Poplar Street became my third home. There was my mom's trailer, my grandmother's house, and the trap, and the way things were going, my mom's trailer didn't really feel like a home at all. But the trap? Shit. There might as well have been a school picture of me hanging off one of the chain-link fences over there because Poplar Street was *home*.

It didn't take long for me to find a crew either. It was me and a couple of the other young guys out there, and we took over one of the abandoned houses and set up shop. We'd have our little stash hidden in the walls and whenever we wanted to get off the block for a minute, we'd go in there and kick it. It was like a clubhouse-slash-trap-house kind of thing because we were still so young and new to the game.

Well, one day we were over there, and we had a little fire going just trying to stay warm when one of our guys busted in mad as hell. Let's call him Marky Mark.

"This motherfucker!" he said, as he stormed through the door.

Marky Mark and I were about the same age, but he'd been in the game for a minute and he was one of the first young cats I knew who really had that dope-boy swag. He was a good dude, and he taught me a couple of things early on about how to carry yourself and how to move.

I'd never seen him that mad before so of course immediately I'm thinking like, are we about to fight? Was somebody about to start shooting up the place? We about to run?

"Shit, goddamn," I said. "What's going on?"

He started pacing all over that tiny-ass house, steaming.

"This motherfuckin' junkie shorted me, Lil' J!" He held up a fist full of crumpled-up bills like I could tell how much he had in his hand. "He shorted me!"

He kept pacing, fuming. "Gave me eight for a ten! But I don't take no shorts!"

He walked over and threw the money in the fire, and as soon as he did that, I hopped up out the little chair I'd been sitting on, like, "Yo! What the fuck?"

I don't know if I thought I was about to try to pull that money out of the fire or what, but I had no idea where his head was at, and I wanted to be ready for his next move. But it seemed like that calmed him down, and he just stood there watching the fire burn.

"I don't take no shorts," he said, finally, like he'd proven his point.

"Man, but you're just going to burn it like that?" I asked him. I still didn't get it. "Eight dollars is better than nothing, right?"

"Nah," he said. "My price is my price. And I don't take no shorts."

Honestly, that blew my mind, but at the same time, I respected it and took his position to heart. For him, it wasn't about the money; it was about the principle. It was about getting what you asked for— what you *deserved*—out of every single deal. The way he was looking at it, you had to have standards and hold yourself and everybody you're doing business with to those standards, otherwise what are you even standing for? He'd lost $2 on that deal, but what if the next time he lost $20 or $200 or $2,000 or $200,000?

I don't think any of us were about to lose $200,000 working out of that little trap house, but even at a young age, Marky Mark knew just how quickly things can add up once you start letting shit slide. And believe me, I've seen it, too. Those deals get bigger, and those numbers start growing, and the next thing you know, those shorts you're taking on the margins just might be able to pay your mortgage or buy you some land. That's not to say you can't compromise, but you've got to know your limits, so when you get into those negotiations, it's one thing to bend a little, it's another to break. At the end of the day, you can't compromise yourself, and you've got to know your worth.

My price is my price. I don't take no shorts.

There is another side to that coin, though, and you've got to be able to see that, too. Just because you've got your principles doesn't mean everybody's going to get on board, and when you stick to your guns and draw that line, some deals will fall apart. And sometimes they'll be deals you really want to do, too. But that's the thing about having principles: they also come with a price.

■ ■ ■

One day not too long after that, I was getting a ride to school with my Auntie Mother and when we pulled past Poplar Street I saw a lot of police activity going on. Even though that was the trap, that type of activity definitely wasn't the norm.

Auntie Mother sucked her teeth, and when she saw me staring out the window in the backseat she was like, "You know that boy, Mark, who used to always be hanging out over there?" She caught my eye in the rearview. "You know him, right, Lil' J? He's about your age?"

I was like, "Yeah, I know him, why?"

"A junkie shot him last night right in the head," she said.

I couldn't believe it, but you know how the 'hood goes. Auntie Mother already knew the whole story. "They said the junkie got in the car with him and they got to arguing over some money and the junkie shot him right there in the car."

I was stunned. "He's dead?"

"Oh, yeah," she said, locking eyes with me. "He's dead."

I didn't say much after that. I didn't say much for the rest of the day, really. I just couldn't wrap my head around it. I mean, I knew what we'd been doing was "bad," but—and I know this sounds crazy—at the time, I never thought anything bad would ever come of it. Maybe we'd get into some trouble at school or the cops would try to bust us up, but to be honest, even if the cops did get involved, I wasn't sure they'd even actually take us to jail. Hawkinsville was so small, we knew all the police!

I definitely didn't think any of us would ever end up dead. But that's exactly what happened to Marky Mark. He'd been standing up to his principles—*my price is my price*—and he'd paid the ultimate cost.

On a certain level I respected it, even then, but I hated losing my friend.

■ ■ ■

"Shit, I'm glad it wasn't me."

That's what this cat Silk used to say whenever something bad happened to somebody in the 'hood. Silk was one of the older hustlers, and what's crazy was before he became a hustler, he was a junkie. I'm talking a straight-up crackhead, for real. He got locked up and when he came home, he was clean and fit, and he had this vision of becoming the man on the other side of the game. I've got to give it up to him because Silk manifested the shit out of that vision, too.

I got to know him a little from hanging out at the basketball courts—Silk could really hoop—but we didn't really get cool until I started hitting the block. Poplar Street was Silk's turf. He owned a couple of the abandoned shotgun homes and lived in a duplex at the end of the road, and pretty much everybody out there was working for him. Over time, he became something like a mentor to me.

Back then, I used to always ride around on my bike, just like I did in Japan. Matter of fact, that was one of the secrets of my early success. When everybody else was standing on the corner waiting for the customers to pull up on the block, I'd be out on my bike catching cars before they even made that turn. That's how I really got on.

Every now and then, I'd pull up at Silk's house, drop my bike in his yard, and we'd roll something up and smoke. I used to sit there and listen to him talk. Well, I'd sit there and listen to him talk and try to holler at the sister of this chick that was living with him at the time, but that was a whole other thing.

As for those smoke sessions, I was really just trying to soak up some game. I'd ask him everything I could think of about getting money and leveling up. Sometimes, I'd keep my mouth shut and just listen, watch, and learn. He taught me a lot in those early days, about all types of things. But whenever I'd bring up something like, *Yo, did you hear about so-and-so and what happened with such-and-such?*, he'd always say the same thing:

"Shit, I'm glad it wasn't me."

I'll admit, that used to feel so cold to me, like, *Damn, Silk—that man is gone.* But by the time I was in my early twenties, I understood. When you're really deep in the game, only one or two weeks go by without you getting a call from someone talking about, *Yo, did you hear about so-and-so and what happened with such-and-such?* It gets to the point where if the phone hasn't rung in a minute, you just start preparing yourself for the call because you know it's going to come. That's a big part of the game.

Our people get slaughtered every day, and when you're young like I was when we lost Marky Mark, you almost don't even fully realize just how deep it goes and how persistent and relentless it is. It's like you don't know any better because you're still looking at life through kids' eyes, so you don't fully understand the consequences are that real and it's hard to process the idea that someone is truly gone. But when it starts happening every day or every week with no breaks, it can be overwhelming. So you've got to find some kind of way to cope or you'll never be able to function.

The truth is, all of that grief, mourning, and healing takes energy and time, so you just become numb to it. It's a survival instinct, almost. What else are you supposed to do? You can only lose so many people before your attitude just becomes, "Shit, I'm glad it wasn't me."

CHAPTER FOUR

Come Shop Wit Me

One day I was at Auntie Mother's house, kicking it with Black. He was back taking another hiatus from Atlanta, and I was sitting in the kitchen watching him break up some weed. He probably had about a thousand dollars' worth, which he was splitting into these little $20 sacks and then stuffing them into a giant Ziploc, so he had something like a couch pillow full of weed.

He already knew I was moving around a little bit here and there. He didn't know everything I was into—like, he didn't know I was selling rocks—but he knew I was into something.

"Hey, cuz, you think you might be able to do something with this?" he asked me when he was done.

Aside from the incident with that bag from the crib, I'd built up a reputation in my family as being someone you could trust to hold something for you if you had to go out of town, so I figured that's what he wanted.

"Nah," he said when I asked. "I was wondering if you might be able to sell it."

When I brought the money back to him, he broke me off a little something. It wasn't much—maybe eighty dollars, if that—but I was so hungry I probably would have done it for less. As long as I was making progress, I didn't care. We started rocking from there.

He gave me another Ziploc bag full of weed, and I sold that. Then he gave me another, and I sold that. Then he gave me another. Then, when my cousins saw I had some other things going on as well, let's just say we diversified my portfolio. I started out small, but slowly and surely, I built myself up.

I didn't know it back then, but they were making top dollar off me, charging me all types of numbers for product that was so stepped on, I'm surprised I was able to sell it at all. All I knew was that they had it, I wanted it, and I could sell it as long as I put in the work.

Day and night, night and day. On the block, on my bike, posted up on the corner of Poplar Street or with Gold Mouth in his car overnight—wherever, whenever, whatever. I was constantly serving, hustling nonstop. I'd be out working all night, run home and sleep for maybe an hour or two, and then go to school in the same clothes I'd had on the night before. As soon as school was out, I was right back on the block doing my thing.

I didn't care what people thought about me, I didn't care if I was getting enough sleep, I didn't care if I was eating right—none of that. As long as I was making money and getting closer to my goals, I was good.

No matter what it took, I was determined to build an empire.

■ ■ ■

Right around then was when I put myself on a meal plan. At the time, Subway had a lunch special: six-inch tuna sub with chips and a drink for $1.99. Subway was about a mile and a half away from the block, so every day I'd bike over there, get lunch, and then bike right back.

For me, it was an easy way to keep a sharp eye on my costs. If I made a hundred dollars a day, spent two dollars on lunch, and ate the rest of my meals at home, I knew I could put away ninety-eight dollars at the end of the day. I knew it would take that type of discipline if I ever really wanted to reach my goals, and I lived like that for years.

Instead of going to the mall and buying three pairs of Jordans every week like other hustlers my age, I'd buy one pair a month and set them aside so I could pop out and get fresh when the time came. Same thing with haircuts and clothes. Instead of hitting the barbershop every day, I'd let my hair go all week, pull up to the mall on Saturday and get right, and keep it moving from there. The rest of the week, it was work clothes, old tennis shoes, and six-inch tuna subs.

I didn't want to spend all my money on a whole lot of extra shit just to impress. I picked that up from hanging around the old heads. A lot of younger cats aren't typically interested in what the older generation has to say, but that was never the case with me. I'd sit on my grandmother's porch for hours and listen to her talk. It was the same thing when we'd barbecue in her front yard after church. All my aunties and uncles, family friends, and neighbors would be over there, and I'd roam around the yard from conversation to conversation, ears open, soaking it all up.

Gathering all that information was exciting to me, and I learned early on that if you listened closely to what people were saying, you could uncover a whole lot of gems. I think that's why some of the people in my family thought I was slow. Instead of running my mouth just to run it, I studied their moves so I could pick up clues on how to get ahead in life and in the game.

Being smart with your money was one of the big things that jumped out at me early on. In the 'hood, everybody was trying to find ways to scrimp and save. You know how they say a dollar saved is a dollar earned? In that type of environment, a dollar saved was like ten dollars earned; everybody's money was so short that stacking any type of savings was a win. After hearing enough people talk about how they were working all these hours and still struggling to feed their families, being frugal just became a big part of who I was.

Another thing I picked up on real quick: ain't nothing cool about going to jail. That's not to take anything away from anybody who's sitting down right now or who already did time—our people get locked up all the time for all types of shit, and not always for legitimate reasons either. If you did your time or you're doing time and you stayed solid, I salute you. We all know there ain't nothing easy about going down that road.

But that perspective only comes with experience. When you're young and coming up in the 'hood, going to jail is almost like a badge of honor. Someone would get caught up and go do a short stretch and when they'd come home, they'd be that dude. Like, he'd earned his stripe. But if you spend enough time around older cats who've done serious time and hear what really goes on in the penitentiary and the toll it takes on your family and your relationships, I promise you your attitude will change. Going to jail isn't cool. It's something you've got to watch out for and avoid.

That was the type of game I was getting from being around older cats. I had to be smart with my money, I had to be strategic with my thinking, and I had to be careful. Otherwise, I ran the risk of hustling backward on top of everything else, and I refused to go in reverse.

■ ■ ■

Auntie Mother's house was perfect.

For one, I'd been going over there since I was a kid so I knew the place inside and out. Two, all the neighbors knew me. I was Lil' J,

Jay Wayne's kid. I might have been in and out of trouble, but for the most part my reputation was solid, and everybody knew I'd never been straight up out in the middle of the street actin' a fool.

They all knew Auntie Mother, too, and her reputation was fierce. She'd always been a little wild, but after she had a brain tumor the size of a grapefruit removed when I was in my early teens, she went from a little wild to straight up off the chain. To be honest with you, I think even the police were intimidated by her. No matter what was going on over there—and believe me, between me and my cousins, there was a lot going on—the police never raided her home. Never. I think they knew that if they ever tried to show up, she'd be out in the yard trying to fight the officers, fists up, like, "Goddammit, I just know none of you motherfuckers are about to try to take my ass to jail!"

So with the spot, the neighborhood, and Auntie Mother on my side, all I needed was the clientele, and Auntie Mother's house was perfect for that, too. There was always something going on over there, with all types of people coming in and out, and then every weekend she'd host these legendary card games. She'd spend all day cooking up a storm and from the moment the factories let out until the sun came up, there'd be a parade of people coming through her door looking to eat, drink, smoke, talk shit, and play cards.

I even had a stash house next door. My man Mel Man's family lived right behind Auntie Mother's house, and we'd grown up together so we were super cool. His upbringing was a lot different from mine. His mom worked at the bank and his family was way more respectable and middle class. He was real laid-back and chill— not all the way 'hood like I was—and if you met him out somewhere, he seemed like somebody you could trust.

Matter of fact, that's how he ended up getting his name. Years later, when we were deep in the game, he was the guy who would take something from one place to the next, and no matter the weather, roadblocks, or problems with the pickup or whatever, he was going to be right where he was supposed to be, on time, with that package in hand. Just like the mailman. Or: Mel Man.

Honestly, Mel Man wasn't even trying to hustle like that. He had hoop dreams when we were coming up. The street dreams were mine. And if I could go back and do it all over again, I would have told him, *Yo, Mel, don't follow me down this road.*

But it went the way it went, and with Mel Man's family's house right there and only a chain-link fence separating his bedroom window from Auntie Mother's backyard, I realized I could hold my stash. That way, whenever my supply ran low, I could dip out into the backyard, knock on Mel Man's window and he could reach through the fence and pass me bags so I could re-up.

That's how I turned Auntie Mother's house into my trap.

■ ■ ■

It was jumping from day one.

As usual, Auntie Mother was in the kitchen, cooking up a storm with pork chops, fried chicken, mac 'n' cheese, and collard greens all on the stove.

"Oh, you're getting it in, huh?" I said, when I walked in.

She was like, "Nice night like this? Shit, I'm expecting a crowd."

I asked her if she needed anything, but Auntie Mother was a pro. "Nah, I'm good, thanks," she said. Then she checked in on me. "You good?"

I'd been dabbling at her place the past couple of weeks, so she knew what I was up to. The whole family did, really. But whereas I'd usually post up and make a couple of plays early in the evening and bounce, that night I was planning on working the whole game.

I'd spent the afternoon stashing bags all over the house so I wouldn't have a lot of shit on me in case the cops decided that night was the night they finally made a move. And the whole time I kept thinking, *Man, I wonder if this will work*. The only thing left to do was wait and see.

"Oh, yeah," I told her. "I'm straight."

I left her in the kitchen and stepped out onto the porch. Auntie Mother was right. You could tell it was going to be one of those nights. Early spring, clear skies, all the kids out playing in the street, the neighbors out in their yards talking and barbecuing, and all that. Summer was coming, and the air just had that feeling like, anything is possible. I was banking on it.

I checked my pockets. Pistol in my left. Sacks in my right. Then I settled into one of the little porch chairs to wait. I didn't have to wait long.

■ ■ ■

I swear over a hundred people must have pulled up that night, and it felt like every single one of them wanted to holler at me. It was a blur, nonstop, like:

"Let me get a ten."

"Let me get a twenty."

"Let me get another. Nah, make it two."

By the time the sun was coming up, I was exhausted but I knew I'd made a killing. I just didn't know how much.

I ducked into one of the empty bedrooms, and emptied my pockets onto the bed to do my count. I separated everything out into neat stacks. Ones, fives, tens, twenties, and so on, all faceup and lying the same way. Then, I started counting, and every time I hit $1,000, I threw a rubber band on it and set it aside.

It took me over an hour to do my count, and when I was done I had fifteen racks sitting right there on the bed. It was the most money

I'd ever made in one night, and I stepped back to take it in. My mind started racing.

If I can make this much in a night, could I make $30 grand in a weekend? Better yet, how much could I make in a week? Or a month? Or a year?

I started replaying the night in my head, looking for ways to improve. Who had I talked to? Who'd wanted what, when? Were there spots where I might have slipped up and lost a sale? The voice in my head kept going. *How can I be more efficient? How can I go harder? How can I get even more done? How can I be* relentless?

I was back out on Auntie Mother's front porch the very next night, and the night after that, and the night after that, and the night after *that*. Even though she didn't host card games every night, I was still making sales. More importantly, I was building up the spot, and people started to know that if you wanted to come see me, you could find me posted up on Auntie Mother's front porch with plenty of product on deck ready to serve.

Over the next few years, I went from hustling a couple rocks on Poplar Street to running a Fortune 500 company on my auntie's front porch. And I played it so low-key hardly anyone knew, because no matter how much money was coming in, I kept my routine. Haircut once a week, couple pairs of Jordans a month, six-inch subs for lunch.

Even when I cut out the middleman and started dealing with the plug directly, I still didn't ball out. And when the big homies from out of town started coming to see me about getting some weight, I'd always tell them the same thing: "Cool, lemme go talk to my people." What they didn't know was that *my people* was me.

It didn't take Auntie Mother long to catch on to what was going on, though, and when she found out how much money I was making, she popped me right in the nose.

I was in her kitchen, cooking up my cousins' recipe—and I'm not talking soul food, either—when, *bop!*

"Shit, goddamn! What the fuck?" Auntie Mother could throw a punch.

She was like, "Motherfucker, I don't know what the hell you think you're doing sitting on my front porch getting rich, and you're not going to cut me in! You can take your ass right on back to your momma's place or wherever you want to go with that nonsense thinking you're not going to pay me, shit. So what is it, Lil' J, you got some money for me or what?"

"Goddamn, you didn't just want to talk to me first?" I asked her, trying to keep the blood dripping from my nose from falling in the pot.

"We're talking now, aren't we?"

That was Auntie Mother. Straight up off the chain. We sat down and worked it all out and we became business partners after that. She kept up the front and I ran the trap, and for a while, the money kept stacking up.

■ ■ ■

By the time I was seventeen, I was young and thuggin' for real. I had so much money coming in, I'd filled up the biggest safe I could find at Walmart, and I was burying money in paint buckets all over the yard. The trap was booming and everything was going according to plan, but at the same time, I was *stressed*.

This was the early-to-mid-nineties and nobody was talking about anxiety disorders, especially not in the 'hood, but looking back, I know that's exactly what was going on with me. I was in way over my head.

On the one hand, I was proud of all the money I was bringing in because it made me feel like I was really doing something with my life. And I was able to put it to good use, too. I was helping my mom make the payments on her trailer and giving money to my grandmother and my sister, and then there was all the money everybody I was working with was making. To me, that was what it was all about—making everybody's lives better and spreading the wealth.

But then, I couldn't stop thinking about everything that could go wrong either. Like, what if the police pulled up? Or some junkie tried to take me out? Or my supply ran dry? Or those paint buckets leaked? Or somebody kicked in my grandmother's door and tried to get in the safe? Or . . . ? Or . . . ?

It got so bad, I was even worried about becoming a junkie my damn self, especially after my man taught me how to cook. I'd be in the kitchen with him for hours and then I'd go to school feeling crazy. My mind would be racing, my heart pounding, and I just knew I was becoming an addict by being around all those fumes.

Matter of fact, I got so paranoid about it that one day, when I was fifteen, I ripped a page out of the back of my grandmother's yellow pages and called a 1-800 drug hotline from one of the pay phones at school.

When the person on the other end picked up talking about, "Hi, you've reached . . ." I damn near whispered into the phone, like, "Hey, listen, so I've been around some people, right? And, uh, they've been . . . Like, I've been in the kitchen with them, you know, with, like, lots of fumes and, uh, I'm really worried that I might be getting addicted to drugs. Like, how would I know? Can you tell me how I'd know?"

I swear my heart was beating so fast I thought it was about to jump right out my chest. Just talking a little bit about what was going on made me feel like the cops or my teachers or somebody was going to come snatch me up, right then and there. And when the guy on the line started asking me all these questions about my parents and who my guardians were, I got so nervous I just hung up the phone and walked away.

That's how bad it was in those early years. I didn't know where to turn, and whenever my anxiety would get real bad, I just assumed it was the withdrawal symptoms kicking in. I told myself I was doing it big, but the truth is I was still a kid, and I wasn't emotionally equipped to handle what I was actually getting into.

One of my biggest fears was that I'd have one moment of weakness, and the next thing I'd know, I'd be out on the block, lost. I'd seen it happen before. I'd be hustling with somebody one day, and then a couple of weeks later, I'd see that same cat out there, trying to cop.

And it wasn't just guys I'd hustled with either. I'd seen family members and close friends get strung out and struggle with addiction, so I carried that fear with me for a long, long time. Even years later, when I was out on the road making moves, hustling state to state, and staying in all of those Motel 6s and Days Inns, I'd be lying there with them things tucked under the mattress, inches from my head, thinking, *What if tonight's the night I let myself slide?*

I never did, though—not even to this day. Despite everything I've seen and all the opportunities I've had, I've never tried it. That's how I know my mind is strong. But back then, I really felt like my mind was starting to break. And the only way I knew how to beat back that feeling was to just keep working. I was speeding down the highway with no brakes, knowing it was only a matter of time before I crashed, praying to God every day that He would give me the strength to hold on just a little longer.

And then I got locked up.

CHAPTER FIVE

I Need a Vacation

You didn't want to go to Alto. I knew that much. Everybody did.

"Alto" is Arrendale State Prison up in Alto, Georgia, which is about an hour north of Atlanta. It's a female prison now, but back when I was coming up, it was all boys and men. That's where they sent the kids they'd charged as adults. And it was notorious.

You'd hear stories about cats getting raped, beat down, cut up in the showers, and all that. And these were kids I'm talking about. Juveniles. I'm telling you, Alto was no joke. Cats would go up there kids and come home hardened criminals.

Well, after me and the homies tried to rob one of the numbers ladies in the 'hood, that's where they were talking about sending me.

I'll be honest, that was one of the dumbest things I ever did. Or ever tried to do, that is.

Now, if you don't know about the numbers game, it's basically like the lottery in the 'hood. Both of my grandmothers ran numbers on the side, but of course we didn't try to rob them. Instead, we tried to rob the numbers lady who lived right next door to my homeboy's crib. And when I say right next door, I mean that literally. You could look out his window and into her house and see her right there.

Well, because we were young and dumb and still getting into all types of young and dumb shit, one Friday night about six of us pulled up in front of her house, jumped out the car with our little ski masks on, and tried to lay her ass down.

We busted in her house with our guns drawn like, "Get on the ground! Get on the ground!"

And I swear that little old lady pulled out that big-ass .357 so quick! Man, we weren't ready for that. As soon as we saw it, we grabbed what we could and ran right back out the door. And of course, the 'hood is so small it didn't take long for word to get back to my mom and the next time I saw her, she was screaming at me like, "Lil' J, keep this up and your ass gon' end up in jail!"

I knew she was right, too, because it wasn't like that was the first time I'd been caught up in some shit either. For years, I'd been in the middle of something. Stealing cars from the school parking lot, getting into fights, jacking car stereos. I was failing classes left and right and constantly getting held back in school. Kids I knew were getting killed, shot and all that, one time with me right there in the car. Like I said, I was in way over my head.

Eventually, I was given a choice. I could go to Alto or I could go to this new thing the National Guard had set up called the Youth Challenge Program, which was basically like boot camp for troubled teens.

Alto or boot camp? Shit, that was a no-brainer.

I was like, "Boot camp! I'll take it, no problem. I'll be there!"

■ ■ ■

In the spring of 1995, my dad dropped me off at Fort Stewart army base just outside of Savannah, and as soon as I got there, I felt like I'd made a mistake. Not that I should have gone to Alto instead—hell no—but that I should never have put myself in the position of having to choose between the two in the first place because the Youth Challenge Program was no joke.

From the moment you stepped on base, the drill sergeants were on your ass.

"Welcome to Fort Stewart, maggots! What were you expecting, a welcome wagon? Well, welcome to hell!"

It was like that nonstop. From five thirty in the morning until lights out, it was jumping jacks, five-mile runs, cleaning the barracks, studying, then more cleaning, more running, and more studying. And those drill sergeants never let up.

"Goddamn, Jenkins, you run slower than my grandmother walks! You want to be out here all day? You better run, Jenkins! Run!"

I was seventeen, and in my eyes I was already a man in the streets, but I learned real quick not to even think about talking back. Say something or get out of line, and it wouldn't just be you that suffered. They'd have the whole platoon running extra miles or out doing push-ups in full fatigues in the rain, with everybody mad at *you*. I'll tell you what, that shit worked, and it didn't take long for everybody to start acting as a unit.

When I first got there, I mostly kept to myself, and I spent a lot of lonely nights lying in my bunk listening to 'Pac in my headphones. *Me Against the World* had just come out and "Dear Mama" was so deep to me that I kept running it back, over and over again. I didn't know it then, but I was really depressed, and I shed so many tears listening to that one song.

■ ■ ■

One day at lunch, all the guys started talking about how much they missed smoking weed. You know how that goes with cats who love to smoke. It was weed this and weed that, the way starving people talk about food, like, "Man when I get out of here, I'm gon' get a pizza and some steak and some wings . . ."

Except with this, it was, "Man, when I get out of here, I'm gon' buy up all the Swisher Sweets in the state and smoke an ounce a day for a year!"

Everybody was going around the table talking about how much they loved getting high, when one of the kids was like, "What about you, Jenkins? You smoke Optimos or Sweets?"

I was like, "Man, I don't even really like smoking like that."

The whole table lit up in disbelief.

"What?"

"Hold up, you don't smoke?"

"Bro!"

Everybody was looking at me like I was nuts, so I figured, *Shit, I guess I might as well tell them a little something about me.*

"Man, so the last time I smoked, right?" I said, looking around the table, "I was with one of my partners . . ."

Then I told them how one night I'd been out riding around with Gold Mouth on the way to the club, when I rolled up a Sweet with some weed I'd bought off one of my cousins earlier in the day. This wasn't one of the Atlanta cousins; this was a different one. That's one thing about my family, at a certain point everybody was hustling some type of way.

So, boom, Gold Mouth was driving like he always was because I didn't get my license until much later on, and as soon as I lit up the blunt, it just started popping and sparking and shit. I figured it must just be some seeds I missed when I was rolling up, so I took a couple hits and kept it moving. We were listening to 'Pac's *Strictly 4 My N.I.G.G.A.Z.* and I was zoning out, high as hell, but then, right when I was about to spark up another blunt, I started to feel like the music was coming to get me. I know that sounds crazy, but that's how I was feeling. Like the music itself was about to come out the speakers of Gold Mouth's Oldsmobile and snatch me up and drag me off somewhere I didn't want to go.

I started freaking out, and yelled over the music, "Pull over! Pull over!"

As soon as the car stopped, I jumped out and started walking up and down the side of the road, trying to get my wind.

Gold Mouth got out to check on me. "Aye, Lil' J, you all right, bro?"

I told him, "Man, I don't know what's going on, but I feel like I'm having a heart attack or some shit. I think I need a hospital."

He looked at me skeptically. "For real?"

I tried to shake the feeling but every time I thought it was fading, it would just come back ten times worse. "Man, for real."

We got back in the car and Gold Mouth peeled off from the curb. He didn't smoke, but I guess he was feeling like, *Ain't no way my cousin is about to die on my watch*, because he raced straight over to Taylor Regional, hopped out, and ran inside to get some help. Meanwhile, I opened the door and damn near fell smack on the ground like Leonardo DiCaprio on some *Wolf of Wall Street* shit.

I started praying. *Please, God, just let me get through this. I swear I'll never smoke again, please!*

When the EMTs finally came out to get me, they hooked me up to some oxygen right there on the ground and started asking me all these questions, trying to make sure I knew my name and where I was. Slowly but surely, I came back around, and when I looked over at Gold Mouth, he burst out laughing, like, "Yo, cuz, you should have seen your face! *I'm dying, cuz, I'm dying!* I've never seen you that scared."

He wasn't lying, either. I've always been the fearless one in my family, but that whole situation had me scared as hell.

When we got back to my grandmother's house, we posted up in the driveway and I started running through the whole night. That's when I remembered: the last time I'd seen my cousin, I'd been over at my grandmother's house, cutting up some rocks on the kitchen table, when she'd walked in and asked if she could buy the shake.

In the 'hood it was common to take all those little leftover crumbs and give them to a junkie to get things done, like if you wanted to borrow their car for a minute or get your car washed, things like that. I figured that's what my cousin was thinking, but sitting in Gold Mouth's car it dawned on me, like, "Yo, I gave her my shake!"

"Hold up, you think she put it in the weed?" he asked me.

I told him, "Man, I *know* she put it in the weed."

He laughed. "Lil' J, the crackhead!"

I was like, "Man, don't even say that shit, cuz. That's not me."

She never did confirm or deny that that's what happened, but to this day I'm convinced that's how it went down. That ended up being a real life-changing experience for me, too, because it made me really want to find a way out of the streets. After that, I was even more paranoid about becoming addicted. I just knew that now that I'd tried it, even by accident, it was only a matter of time before I'd slip up, give in, and end up being Lil' J the crackhead for real.

When I finished telling the story everybody at the table was like, "Goddamn, bro, she did you like that?" And asking me questions like, "What was it like?" and all that.

Then from the end of the table, one of the other kids who hadn't really said anything was like, "Man, I had that same thing happen to me."

I was surprised that anyone had been through a situation like that, so I asked him about it, and when he finished telling his story he was like, "Fucked me up, too, so I don't really smoke like that anymore either."

After that, me and him sort of hit it off. His name was Demetrius Ellerbee, but if you know anything about me or have ever listened to my music or followed my career, you probably know him by another name—Kinky B.

■ ■ ■

The Youth Challenge Program wasn't all morning runs, cleaning the barracks, and jumping jacks in the rain. There were life skills courses and leadership training, and they had us do community service and taught us about civics and nutrition. They also offered a pathway to a GED, and that was a big thing for me.

Going in, I'd told myself, *If I don't get anything else out of this, at least let me get my GED.*

That was the deal I'd made with everyone else, too. My mom, my dad, my grandmother. Even the people down at the sheriff's office. That was one of the conditions of me being at Fort Stewart in the first place. If I got kicked out of the program or failed to get my GED, they were sending my ass to Alto with no questions asked.

When they put the deal on the table my dad was like, "This is your chance, Lil' J. You better take advantage of it before it's too late."

It wasn't that I wasn't smart. I was just way, way behind in school because I could never seem to focus when I was there. Whenever I was in class, I was always thinking about all the other things going on, like, *Where am I going to sleep tonight? I wonder if one of my uncles is going through my things. Are we going to have enough food to eat? Do I have enough clothes? How am I ever going to get out of this situation I'm in and get some real stability and bread?*

Being at Fort Stewart finally gave me time and space to set those concerns aside for a minute and apply myself to doing what I needed to do. In the end it wasn't even all that hard, and when the day came, I walked into the testing room feeling like money. My confidence was high, my uniform was hard pressed, and my boots were shining. The program was coed, and I'd be lying if I said there weren't at least a couple of girls I was trying to impress in the room, so I had that motivating me, too.

When they posted the results and I found my name and saw I'd passed, that wave of emotion was something else. I was proud, excited, relieved, and then proud and excited and relieved all over again. I was even almost a little sad just knowing how much it would mean to my mom. I'd really done it, and it said so right there on the board—*J. Jenkins: pass.* I wasn't a lost cause.

Then, I saw Kink staring at his name–*D. Ellerbee: fail.*

He looked so sad, I told him, "Yo, man, if you want, I could really help you with this shit for real."

■ ■ ■

Kink and I became bunkmates after that, and we'd stay up every night talking after lights out. I'd help him study and he'd tell me stories about what it was like coming up where he was from—Macon, Georgia, a small city about an hour north of the 'Ville.

Kink was from Macon's west side, and he was a Duncan Blocc Gangsta Crip. I didn't know anything about gang life back then, but I knew about life in the 'hood and everything he was talking about sounded familiar to me. The details were a little different, of course, but the outline was the same, and the more we talked the closer we became.

When I look back on the three months we shared that bunk, I always think about that scene in the movie *Blow* when Boston George and Diego Delgado are sharing a cell. Diego tells George,

"You have a dream. And maybe you will accomplish it. But yet, you failed. Why?"

George is like, "Because I got caught."

"Naw, 'manito," Diego says. "You failed because you had the wrong dream."

Talking to Kink, I realized it was the same thing with us. We weren't in the Youth Challenge Program because we got caught. We got caught because we had the wrong dream.

We'd been thinking small, and even though we both dreamed of making it out and making it big, neither one of us really had a plan. I had the outlines of one—hustle, save, and stack my bread—but I wasn't sure I could see it all the way through, and in the meantime, I was still getting caught up doing dumb shit like trying to rob the numbers lady on the side.

Every day in the 'hood brought more temptations, more risks, and more tests, and until I went through that program, I knew it was only a matter of time before I failed. I'm not talking about *failed* like getting sent to Fort Stewart for six months. I'm talking about getting strung out, sent up to Alto, or worse. And for what? Sneaker money? To look cool at the club? To get a rep?

Nah, that was the wrong dream. And I don't know I ever would have realized it either if I hadn't gone away when I did. Those six months at the Youth Challenge Program gave me an opportunity to get some distance from the 'hood, gain some perspective, reset, and take stock of who I was and where I was trying to go. I know they weren't necessarily trying to train us to be the best hustlers we could be—okay, I know they *definitely* weren't trying to train us to be that—but I learned some invaluable lessons while I was there that I still carry with me to this day.

1. **You have to take the time to reset, especially when you're stressed.** I know that can be hard at times, especially when

you're really going through it, but if you can get a little separation and shake up your daily routine, you'll be surprised by how your perspective will change.

2. **Success only comes from discipline, dedication, persistence, and commitment.** If you're not fully committed to your goals from the outset and willing to do whatever it takes day in and day out to achieve them, you're destined to fail because half-stepping won't get it done. So make a plan, lace up, set your sights, and follow through.

As for Kink and his GED? He passed.

He was so happy when he did and so grateful for my help that I think that's what really cemented our friendship. It was one of those early instances that showed me that I had leadership skills that I didn't know I had. I was seventeen with a sixth-grade education, if that. Now we both had our GEDs, and that had a whole lot to do with me.

■ ■ ■

That good feeling didn't last. Matter of fact, the closer we got to the end of the program, the worse I felt. Typically, in that type of situation you can't wait to get home, but for me it was the opposite. My dad had been right—the Youth Challenge Program had been as much of an opportunity as a punishment. Even more than that, though, it had been an escape.

For six months, I'd been able to leave the 'hood behind, get out of my daily routine, and really work on myself. But the 'hood was still the 'hood, and I knew the same problems I'd left were still waiting for me when I came back home. And then some. Right before I'd gone into the program, I'd found out this girl I'd been messing with was pregnant with my son. I'd gotten my GED and I had a little cash set aside, but it wasn't much, and on top of everything else, I was about to be a dad. As the days ticked by and that reality set in, I got more and more depressed.

A week before the end of the program, they took us to Savannah to tour Hunter Army Airfield and check out some of the big battleships they had docked at the port. It was a field-trip-slash-army-recruiting tool, and as they showed us around, they told us all about the day-to-day of being in the service to see if we wanted to sign up. I respected my father for going that route, but I'd seen enough with him to know that wasn't the route for me. I just didn't know what my path would be.

"And this is the USS . . ." *whatever*, the recruiter said as we boarded one of those big-ass boats.

I tuned him out and got lost in my thoughts. It was one of those beautiful, clear days you get on the coast. Huge, crisp sky with a cool breeze coming off the water, the sound of seagulls in the air, and the waves crashing against the side of the boat below.

Still, all I could hear was an endless loop of questions running through my head.

What am I going to do when I get out of here? Am I really going to go right back to living at my grandmother's house? I can't do that forever, right? Do I get a factory job? Do I even want to do that, and would they even hire me if I did? If I don't work, how am I going to help my family? How am I going to survive? How am I going to provide for my son?

Real talk, standing on the deck of that battleship, staring out at the ocean, I felt like I was losing my mind. The only things I could see ahead of me were more challenges, more struggles, more temptations, and more pain. Even surrounded by all that water, I felt like I was standing out in the middle of a desert all alone, dying of thirst.

The way I was looking at it, my future wasn't bright—it was bleak. And when the tour was over and they gave us some time to wander the ship, I walked out to the tip of the boat farthest from land and leaned over the rail. The water was much deeper here, dark and blue, and the waves crashed violently against the boat's steel sides.

I stepped back and looked out at the ocean, stretching out into the horizon until it met the sky. Then I looked back over the rail.

If I jump, it will all be over, I thought to myself. *No more responsibilities. No more problems. I'll be free.*

I watched the waves crest and break, thundering below.

I bet it would be quick, I thought. *I wonder if it'll hurt.*

I felt so worthless in that moment. All I wanted was a way out of the 'hood, some kind of way to show the world that I had real value and to live the American dream. And I could only think of one way to make it to where I wanted to be, and that path led straight through the streets.

I would never have admitted it to myself, but as depressed as I was in that moment, I was way more scared. I knew what the street life brought because I'd seen it firsthand. At the same time, I knew that even with as much as I'd already seen, I was nowhere near where I wanted to be. Ever since I was young, I'd had this picture of me as a man in my mind's eye—successful, stable, and respected, with the designer three-piece suit, the rose-gold wedding band, and the beautiful wife and kids by my side. Standing there on that boat, feeling like there was only one way for me to get there, I knew things were going to get way, way worse before I ever achieved that dream. And that's if I survived long enough to see it through.

I looked down at the ocean again and time slowed to a crawl. I knew I had a decision to make, and for forty-five minutes I stood there, debating what to do. It felt like I was out there for hours.

Do I jump off this boat or do I dive back into the streets? And if I choose the streets knowing where that leads, would I be better off just jumping off this boat?

Back and forth, back and forth, weighing the pros and cons, trying to decide my fate. I heard the whistle calling us back to the bus blow in the distance. It was now or never. I took one last look over the edge, and then I walked away.

A week later, I was back in the 'hood. And the only thing that had changed was me.

CHAPTER SIX

I-75

'd been home from Fort Stewart for about a month and a half when I called Kink and told him I was thinking about coming up to see him. He was surprised. "What, to Macon?"

"Yeah," I told him. "You gonna be around?"

He was like, "Shit, hell yeah. I ain't going nowhere, come through!"

Three days later, I was headed north on I-75 in a T-Top Cutlass with European fronts I'd bought out of the back of an *AutoTrader* magazine for $3,500. Still didn't have a license, but I had a car, and I felt like a boss eating up that road. When I pulled up on Kink, we went straight to Duncan Blocc so he could give me the lay of the land. What I saw blew my mind.

You would have thought we were in South Central on some *Straight Outta Compton* shit the way everybody was flagged up, and they were gangbanging like you wouldn't believe.

"All right, so you got the Mafia over there," Kink said, pointing to some cats with black flags.

"And they're beefing with these dudes over here," he said, pointing to some other cats rocking a different flag. "And they're beefing with . . ."

He just kept going, talking about how these cats over here couldn't go to that corner store over there because of who controlled what turf. Eventually I was just like, "Hold up, hold up. You're saying that *they* can't go to *that* corner store?"

I pointed at the corner store, which was maybe about fifty yards away.

He was like, "Yeah, nah, they can't go over there. If they do, it's on."

I tried to wrap my head around it, but to be honest, it all sounded a little crazy to me. "So you're telling me y'all are all going to war over who gets to stand where and who gets to shop at which corner store and y'all ain't getting no money?"

"I mean, we're getting a little something," he said.

"Yeah, but Kink, man, c'mon," I said. "I'm talking about *money*."

We sat there in silence for a minute, watching the block. Finally, I was like, "Man, we gotta figure this shit out. Y'all got all this muscle, y'all just ain't got no hustle."

He looked at me. "And you do?"

I told him straight up, "You're fucking right."

That's when I made up my mind. There would be no second-guessing, no giving into temptation, no lack of commitment or focus. I was going to take all the skills I'd picked up at Fort Stewart and everything I'd learned about myself while going through the program, and I was going to apply all of it—1,000 percent—to my hustle. And I was going to be militant about it, too. Nothing and no one was going to stop me from reaching my goals. I was going all in. And I was going to be relentless.

■ ■ ■

A few days later, I dipped back down to the 'Ville to put things in play. My first stop was to go see this older cat who was dating one of my cousins at the time. The streets were dry, but I knew he had a solid connect down in Florida so I thought he might be able to slide me something to hold.

He lived in a trailer out in this area called Devil's Head, and when I pulled up and he asked me what I was looking for, I told him, "Man, I'll take whatever you've got."

I was still at that age—seventeen going on eighteen—where on the one hand I was grown, but on the other, I could tell he was thinking maybe I was still just a kid. Finally, he was just like, "Well, shit. C'mon."

I followed him through his yard to this old, broken-down, rusted-out Oldsmobile sitting on four flats in the middle of some waist-high weeds. He popped the trunk and I swear it was like that scene in *Pulp Fiction* when John Travolta opens the case. There must have been something like twenty grocery bags in there, and every single one of them was full to the brim with these big-ass cookies. I'm talking he had so much shit, it damn near filled the trunk. My eyes lit up.

"Get what you want," he said, like it was nothing.

I reached in and grabbed a whole bag of cookies, like, "Shit. I want *this*."

"Cool," he said. "Now go out there and get it and bring your money back."

And that's exactly what I did. I took that bag to Macon and posted up on Duncan Blocc with Kink and the rest of the homies, and I ended up staying up there for years. I grew a multimillion-dollar business just off of that one decision alone, sitting there in my T-Top Cutlass with Kink, like, *Fuck it, I'm going all in.*

And I never looked back.

■ ■ ■

Real talk, all the shit that went down in Macon could fill a whole other book. There were so many people and so many plays, big business and petty business, stand-up guys and low-down snakes, beefs, wins, losses, and people getting caught up and killed or sent away to do serious time.

And it was never-ending, too, because that's the thing about being a hustler for real. You never get a moment off because as soon as somebody catches you slipping, it's a wrap. So everyday you're just on high alert, keeping tabs on everything—who's holding the money, who's holding the work, are they cool and safe, who else knows what's going on, when's the next shipment coming in, is the plug still straight, and on and on and on.

But I will say this, though. You can pull up on Duncan Blocc right now, and ask anybody out there who put the 'hood on, and to this day they'll tell you "Jeezy," straight up. I'm not saying I'm Tookie Williams or anything like that—definitely not—but everything about me checks out. When I came through, I changed lives, and I changed the block forever.

■ ■ ■

One thing about me: I've always been able to spot an opportunity, and once I see it, I'm willing to do whatever it takes to capitalize on it to the fullest degree. That was true in Russell City, and at the Exchange, and at those little electronics stores in Japan. It was true with that $20 my uncle gave me and that big bag of weed I got from my cousin, and it was true when I was riding my bike up and down Poplar Street and posted up at Auntie Mother's house on the front porch. And it was absolutely true in the Mack, because I didn't just bring in a bunch of work and put on the block. I opened the whole city up, and the only way I was able to do it was by seizing the opportunity I saw right in front of me and going against the grain.

You've got to think, when I first got to Duncan Blocc, it was an all-out war. You had the Bloods over here, the Crips over there, the Mafia over there. Everybody had beef and nobody was really getting any bread. But the way I was looking at it, Business 101 says you want to remove as many barriers as possible so the money flows. The bigger the market, the bigger the opportunity, which gives everybody participating in that market the potential to make way more bread.

The way they were handling things, there were nothing but barriers everywhere you looked. You couldn't stand on this corner, they couldn't stand on that corner, and on and on. That was the culture and I respected it, but at the same time, it wasn't good business.

I used to try to explain it to the homies, too, like, "Okay, I understand the beef, but there has to be some type of understanding we can all come to so we can go get the money, right? Because otherwise, what are we doing everyday taking all these risks?"

Some of them got it, and some of them didn't, but I come from a family of hustlers so that's what I know. Rather than keep talking about how I thought it should go, eventually I just got out and got on my grind.

■ ■ ■

I don't even really remember how I got cool with Dante, but he was from about four blocks over from Duncan Blocc and he was a Blood. Of course, the homies weren't fucking with him because he rocked that red flag, but I'd never had any problems with him so when we started doing our thing, we just had to keep it on the low.

That was even better for me, though, because that was another one of my rules: never let anybody in your game room. I believe that's true generally because information is power, no matter what business you're in. And then when you see all the data harvesting all of these social media companies are doing, that just lets you know information is one of the most valuable commodities in the world.

That's especially true in the streets. As soon as someone finds out what you've got going on, they've got the upper hand. They could set you up, have you robbed, snitch on you, have you killed—or, shit, all of the above. You just never know.

When I was first starting out, my uncle Bo Slick used to always say, "Never let your right hand know what your left hand is doing." Well, you know how they say a drunk ass speaks a sober mind? My uncle Bo Slick sure liked his gin, but I still live by that one to this day. The less people know, the safer it is for everyone. If you follow that, it just might save your life.

As for Dante—or Tay, as everybody called him—he ended up being my direct line to the Pirus over on the south side, which opened up a whole other side of town. We'd meet up in the parking lot of Saleems Fish Supreme and then he'd go over to the south side and get it off. And we were so discreet with it that nobody over there ever even heard my name.

It was the same thing on the east side. There was this cat, Carlos, and when I first got to town, his name was ringing. He was the *man*.

After I'd been up in the Mack for about a year, he pulled up on me and the homies one night when we were kicking it in the parking lot of a gas station after the club. I'd just bought my first Lexus, a GS 400, like the Hot Boys were always rapping about. Carlos leaned out the window of his big-body Benz and hollered at me like, "I heard about what you've been doing. I see you."

Then he said, "Just don't fuck my bitch."

Man, I busted out laughing so hard when he said that, I swear. But when I saw he was serious, I was just like, "Oh, shit, all right. Bet. No problem. We're good."

That was so wild to me, but I guess that was his biggest concern.

Well, maybe a month or so after that, I was trapping out of this shotgun house on the west side when I got the call that Carlos had been shot and killed in his ragtop Buick. Fucked me up, too, because we'd started talking after that night at the gas station and I could tell he was a good dude. When I heard the news, I was just like, "Damn." I could hear Silk's voice in my head: *I'm glad it wasn't me.*

Carlos had been the king of the east side and his death opened up another opportunity—there was room for a new king. I started befriending some cats who were hustling over there, one thing led to another, and eventually I hooked up with this dude whose name I'm not going to say, and we locked in and locked that bitch down. After that, I had the west side through DBGC and them, the south side through Tay, and the east side through my man.

Then, I started messing with this cat Gangsta Cal, who was notorious over on the east side. We were doing our thing there for a minute and then he went off to Houston to try to do something, but that got fucked up and instead of telling me about it, he tried to give me a bag full of Magic City money—nothing but ones.

We'd been doing a lot of business together so I trusted him at the time, but something about that day told me I needed to check the bag. Of course, when I saw all those ones, I immediately started blowing up his phone, and when he didn't answer, I threw my car in gear and went after his ass. I was driving my green Pontiac Grand Am that day. Those Grand Ams were some of my favorite cars because they had a little muscle on them, but they were so low-key you could throw some tint on and blend right in.

I pulled up on his passenger side, held up the bag and yelled, "Yo! What the fuck is this?"

As soon as he saw me, he veered off and merged onto I-75. That's when I knew it was really on. I swerved across traffic and followed him right onto the interstate. We raced down the highway for miles, switching lanes. He's going, I'm going. He's going, I'm going. And I was gaining on him, too.

I pulled up on his driver's side and we were neck and neck on some *Days of Thunder, Ford v Ferrari* shit. Except he wasn't driving no damn Ferrari.

I yelled at him again. "Yo, pull over! Yo!"

Finally, I was just like, fuck it. I reached down, pulled that thing out, and let it spray.

Pop-pop-pop-pop-pop-pop-pop-pop!

Lit up his whole shit in broad daylight, right there in the middle of the road.

He lost control of his car for a second, but I just kept going. From the rearview I saw him pull over to the side. I didn't know if I'd hit him or what, but I wasn't about to stop to check. I wanted my money, don't get me wrong, but I valued my freedom even more.

I pulled off the highway about thirty miles down the road and ended up backing the car into some bushes I found behind an abandoned church. A couple of hours later, one of the homies came and got me, and we stripped everything out of the car and bounced. I never went back.

Things got pretty hectic there for a minute because his people were about their issue and we were definitely about ours, but I refused to let it go. As soon as somebody starts thinking it's cool to take from you, then everybody starts thinking it's cool to take, and of course there ain't nothing cool about that. I put the word out and made sure it was understood, like, "If y'all don't get me my money, y'all ain't never going to be able to sleep because we're going to be on your head."

About a week later, he hit me up, like, "Yo, I got your money," and we made a plan to meet at the mall, and . . .

But, shit, let me just stop right there because I could go on and on. Like I said, everything that happened in Macon could fill a whole other book.

■ ■ ■

I really say all of that just to say this: when I first pulled up on Duncan Blocc, I saw a lot of untapped potential and a market that was being choked off by structural issues that—even though they existed for real reasons—were standing in the way of everybody getting some bread. Nobody had thought to break down those barriers and open the market up the way I did because they were too deep in it. To them, it was what it was.

It took an outsider's perspective to question the accepted way of doing things and to see how big of an opportunity finding another way could be. It was a flip on what the business world calls the Blue Ocean Strategy but applied to the streets, and it was the same thing my cousins had been doing in those small towns all along. Instead of competing for the same blocks as everyone else in Atlanta, they found the blue ocean in the 'Ville and the surrounding areas and got it off. My innovation was to take that same approach to the Mack.

On the ground level, Macon was a red ocean with a whole bunch of sharks swimming around, fighting for food. But above the fray, everything was blue because nobody was trying to lock down the whole town. That's where I came in. I was willing to look above the fray. Maybe a better name for what I was doing would be Blue Sky, but whatever you want to call it, I'll tell you this: it worked.

As for that Gangsta Cal situation, turns out he didn't get hit on the highway that day, but he definitely got the message. And you better believe I got paid in full.

■ ■ ■

So I was dating this girl, right? She was one of the baddest chicks in the city, and she worked at the Lexus dealership, so I'd always have the flyest whips because she'd get them for me right off the lot.

Her husband was locked up down in Florida doing time, and we all assumed he was a hustler. Come to find out, he was one of the biggest cat burglars in the world, no lie. He was the guy who would break in and steal all the family jewels from the heirs to the Ford Motor Company and shit like that. They had stories about him on CNN and all that. Crazy, right?

They had a family together—four kids—and I believe he was serving a life sentence at the time. When we first started dating, I went down to Florida to see him and he gave us our blessing like, "Just make sure my family is straight."

So, boom. At one point, she told me she knew a guy in Macon who was trying to make a play. I was like, "Cool, go holler at my man."

She went to see him and when she was done, she hit me up and told me she thought someone was following her.

"You *think* or you *know*?" I asked her.

"I'm pretty sure," she said. "I've been seeing the same car all day."

I was like, "Shit, well, whatever you do, don't come over here. Don't none of us need any of that."

"All right," she said, "let me see what I can do. I'll call you back."

Of course, my mind was racing as soon as we got off the phone, like, *How much of my stuff is over at her place? If she gets jammed up, will she talk?* And things like that, just stressing.

A couple of hours later, she hit me up, like, "I'm good. They're gone."

I don't know what she did or how she did it, but she was really street-smart and she lost them some kind of way. That's who she was, though. She was a soldier.

After that, she was on me to switch my shit up so we started talking about it a little bit, and then one day I went to meet her for lunch and she was like, "You know, I might know some people down in Florida who could help."

"You sure they're straight?" I asked her.

"Oh, yeah. It's my homegirl's family," she said. "They're straight."

As soon as she got off work, we hit the road, headed straight down I-75 with a duffel bag full of cash. We used to call that a suicide mission because we didn't have a plan. It was just us, the money, her connect, my ambition, and a dream.

When we got to Fort Lauderdale, I got two motel rooms—one for us, one for the bag—and then she took me to meet her people. Her homegirl was a teacher, Jamaican and married to this white dude. They lived in a nice house in a nice neighborhood, and they were cool. And damn near everybody in her homegirl's family was in the game.

Her homegirl introduced me to her brothers, and they took me around the 'hood and showed me all the local spots. Then for days, we were just waiting around to make the play, like, "When's the bag coming? When's the bag coming?"

Whenever we asked, her brothers would always say the same thing. "Soon, man, soon. It's coming. Chill."

Then finally one day, *boom*. They delivered the bag, I delivered the cash, and we immediately rolled out with my girl behind the wheel and me sitting shotgun with the bag on my lap for ten hours straight. No plan, no stash spot. Nothing. Like I said, *suicide*.

After that, those Florida trips became a regular thing, and I mean *regular*. For the next year and a half, we were on the road four or five times a week. She'd get off work and we'd be out, off making plays. When we had it running like clockwork, I started sending my people down on their own and we kept that going for another few years, but even then, I'd always be around, hanging in the cut just to make sure everything was straight.

That's how everybody in Florida got to know me. I was the young cat from Georgia who was always riding through the 'hood in the latest Lexus with all the watches and chains. They didn't know my real name or what I really did, they just knew I was getting money, and for years, a lot of people down there just knew me as "Bling." Some of them still call me Bling to this day. A lot of them switched it up on me after I got famous, though. Now whenever I see them, they're always like, "Yo, it's Michael Jackson Jeezy. What up?!"

■ ■ ■

Eventually, that whole situation fell apart.

My girl's homegirl got jammed up, and then it turned out the feds were sitting on my girl's crib, too. The only way I knew was because they stopped Gold Mouth around the corner from her place one day, right after he'd come to see me. Thank God he was riding clean so they had to let him go, but after that, it was just like, *Man, what the fuck?* Come to find out later on they'd been hiding in the bushes with binoculars, taking pictures and all that, but by the time they closed in on her, I was already out the door.

Those trips down to Florida were a big part of my success, though, there's no denying that. And not just because they opened up so much for me in the streets, either, although that was no small thing. But street money is short money, no matter how much you're bringing in. That's so important, I'll say it again: *Street money is short money, no matter how much you're bringing in.* In the streets, there are so many ways things can go wrong, the only real questions are: *How and when will it go wrong for you?*

I always knew I needed a way out, but it wasn't until I started taking those Florida trips that I finally saw something that looked like it might be the way out for me.

■ ■ ■

S.O.P.

That was the name of the label and the group. It stood for Sounds of Profit, Inc., and when I first met them, they were a bunch of young, cool guys coming straight out of Fort Lauderdale. They were getting it in like I was, but they were trying to make it in the music game, too. They had their own studio and an in-house graphic designer, and they were pressing up their own T-shirts and CDs and trying to get people down with their movement everywhere they went.

In 1999, we all went down to Daytona Beach together for spring break and I got a close look at how they were moving. That trip really opened my eyes. They rented a big-ass Winnebago and had it wrapped with their logo. Then they went and parked right on the beach and spent the whole weekend working their music like they were working the trap. The whole crew was out there all day, every day in matching S.O.P tees with their music blasting, handing out CDs and talking to everybody walking by.

Everything about it was dope to me. My cousins had been involved in the Atlanta music scene for years, but they were way more polished with it working with cats like Jermaine Dupri, Another Bad Creation, Lil' Zane, and them early on because that was the play: find and groom talent and see if they could go pop.

S.O.P wasn't chasing that type of success. Or maybe they were, but the way they were going about it was way more street, and that's the type of shit I was on. My vibe was cats like Tupac, Master P, the Hot Boys, and then Trick Daddy after I started making all those trips.

Being around S.O.P was a revelation to me, because even though we were both in the game, they were working two tracks. I was so inspired that as soon as I got back to the Mack, I hit up Kink like, "Yo, we should start making music."

■ ■ ■

The truth is, I never wanted to be a rapper. Some people are natural-born entertainers and damn near pop out of the womb with a mic in hand, like, "Look, ma, I'm here!"

But that wasn't me. I always wanted to be a CEO.

One of the first things I did when I got back to Macon was go out and find some space in this cheap-ass industrial building on the out-skirts of town. Then, I hit up my cousins and had them come down to help me out. They took me to Guitar Center, and I dropped some-thing like seventy grand all in to get everything you needed for a studio setup back then. I got the DA-88, some ADAT machines, a 24-bus board, mics, amps, cords, stands—all that. My cousins han-dled the build-out, and my cousins being my cousins, it wasn't like they did it out of the kindness of their hearts. They charged me for everything, and years later I realized they'd ran it up on me. At the time, I didn't know, but I also didn't care. I had the bread. What I needed was a way out. So if they said something cost x, then I paid x, no questions asked.

Still, I swear the most important thing I ever bought for that stu-dio wasn't the mics or the mixing board or the studio monitors. It was this gray sofa I got from this furniture spot all the hustlers used to go to in the Mack called Suns. To me, that sofa was like the stamp on the whole situation. In my mind, once that was in there, we were *official* official because now we could treat the studio like the trap and grind nonstop. If anyone got tired or needed a break, they could hit the couch to get some Zs, then get up and take a birdbath in the sink, throw on a fresh black tee, and get right back to work.

As soon as we had the studio, I went all over the 'hood looking for cats who thought they could rap. I wasn't looking for demo tapes or songs I could check out or none of that. I was straight up just looking for anybody on the block who wanted a shot, like, "Yo, you said you wanted to be a rapper, right? Come through."

We'd give them a beat, and if Kink and I liked what we heard, we signed them on the spot. We called ourselves Young Gunz Entertainment. Just like Baby and Slim with Cash Money, and Jay-Z and Dame Dash with Roc-A-Fella Records, Kinky B and I were the co-owners and co-CEOs.

We opened up shop in 1999, and that was a real proud moment for me. I was twenty-one with my own record label, my own studio, and even a private drive that led right up to the studio door. Every day when I'd pull up, I'd walk in and there'd be all these young cats straight off the block in there, making music and chasing the dream—our dream—and it was such an incredible feeling to see it right there in front of my face, manifesting in real time. Me and Kink were going to put the 'hood on the map and we were bringing all the homies with us, too.

■ ■ ■

It didn't take long for that whole situation to go left. For one, my cousins kept running up the numbers and that started to take its toll. There I was trying to change my life and the whole time they're treating me like an ATM. The studio setup was one thing, but where they really got me was when I started talking to them about getting a group we were working with on a compilation mixtape they were putting together.

Shit, if I'd known then what I know now, I damn sure could have saved myself a whole lot of bread. First, we had to pay them just to get a song on the compilation. Then, they said they were going to market the record and that was going to cost. That sounded a little off, but okay, cool. Then, they said they wanted to do some artwork for the tape and that had a price. *Then* they wanted to set up some interviews and they needed some money for that. At that point, it was just like, *Bro, what?* I must have spent a couple hundred grand with them all in, and for nothing, really. To get one song on a mixtape.

Up until then, I'd been feeling good about the whole music thing. I believed in what we were doing, and I knew as long as we kept at it, we would eventually figure it out and break through. But after breaking all of that bread with nothing to show for it, I started to feel the doubt creeping in, like, *Damn, this shit costs a lot of fucking money! How the hell am I going to pull this off?*

One good thing did come out of that situation, though—it showed me how *not* to do it. In that respect, you could say the money I spent with them was almost like my music business school loan, and I learned that if I was ever going to make it in music, I was going to have to find another way.

Then all these other things started happening with our group. One guy got locked up for a double homicide and sentenced to twenty years. Another one caught a separate murder case, so he was out. Then I got into it with one of the other guys over some shit we had going on in the streets, and that kind of tore a hole in the whole situation. You know how they say blood and business don't mix? Yeah, well, business and business don't mix either, especially when it's street business.

Kink wanted to keep things going, but after that to me it was just like, *Man, if I can't trust one of my artists and he's coming to the studio every day, how's that supposed to work?* We gave it a shot for a minute, but that was the end of the group.

By that point I'd spent so much money trying to get on, I decided I might as well get back to getting money for real because I was damn near broke. Then Cuzzo called talking about a new play.

■ ■ ■

I should have known better. Like I said, growing up, my cousins were legends in my family, and they were like superheroes to me. But once I got out there and started moving around on my own, I noticed some things about them that made me question everything I'd thought I'd known.

Like Cuzzo had a little finesse to him, but he was—how can I say this?—*different*. I used to hear things about him and who he was running with here and there, but he's my cousin so I love him and initially that made some things easy to dismiss. Over time, though, I came to realize his word wasn't his bond. Then a couple of things happened, and it was just like, *Man, I can't trust this guy at all*.

For example, one time he hit me up in the middle of the night talking about how he'd run off on some Mexicans and they were talking about shooting up his mom's place in Decatur, the same house I used to visit as a kid.

I grabbed my AK out the closet and rushed over there, and when I pulled up, I saw my cousin and this cat he used to run with who was notorious as the finesse king of Atlanta standing in the front yard with their guns drawn. I hopped out my Monte Carlo and cocked that AK back like, "Where they at?"

Then Cuzzo started telling me the story about how he got this call from these guys and that they knew where his momma stayed and all that, and then all of a sudden it was just like, "Yo, what was that?"

Our ears shot up. Now, you've got to remember it's the middle of the night, and we're in this nice, quiet residential neighborhood. The streets were empty, not a car on the road, with no one out there but us. Then we heard it again.

Crack-crack.

This time there was no mistaking it. There was something moving in the woods.

Man, when I tell you my cousin and his partner took off. You'd have thought they were at the NFL Combine or some shit. They were *gone.* Just left me standing there in his mom's front yard, alone with my AK looking around, like, *What the fuck?*

Turns out it was just his brother, Black, creeping around in the woods behind the house, and those Mexicans never showed, but I never looked at Cuzzo the same after that. To me, it was just like, man, how are you going to call me and get me out my bed and you ain't going to stand on business? What part of the game is that?

To be honest, I should have stopped fucking with him right there, but that's the thing about the trap: it's really easy to get trapped. It doesn't take much to become addicted to getting money, believe me. For me, it started when I doubled up over on Poplar Street, and I kept chasing that high. But that's the thing about addiction, right? Once it's got its claws in you, it's hard to stay away. You'd be amazed at how many people I've known who somehow managed to get out and go legit only to get caught up when they went to make one last play.

With the streets, it takes a kind of wishful thinking to know all the risks and to see people suffer the consequences of taking those risks all the time, and to still go out there and take those same risks every day, like, *Man, that's not gonna happen to me.*

That was me. Stuck in the trap chasing that high, getting money like a motherfucker one minute and going broke the next, which made me want to take even more risks to get back up. So even though I saw my cousin for who he was the night he left me standing in his momma's front yard, when he called and said he might have a play in Atlanta and asked if I might be able to put some money together, I didn't hang up.

Instead, I was just like, "Yeah, I might put something together. What's up?"

. . .

I felt nervous about the whole situation from jump.

On the way to the spot, I kept thinking about the quarter million in my book bag and all the ways things could go wrong. At a certain point, I even said something, too, like, "Aye man, let me go back and get my strap."

He was like, "Man, come on. It's cool. These my people."

As it turned out, that was the problem.

. . .

The deal went down in the cab of a semi truck parked on a residential street over on the west side of Atlanta near the AU Center.

When we got in the truck, there was a plastic laundry basket in the back seat with a blanket thrown on top of it. I peeked under the blanket and saw nothing but gray duct tape. Everything looked right to me. I gave my cousin's guy the bag, took the basket, and bounced, but when I got back to where I was staying and started going through the shit, I realized everything in that basket was fake. I'm talking nothing but Sheetrock and duct tape, no lie. Man, I was ready to explode.

I started blowing up my cousin's phone, but he wasn't answering and that just made it worse. When something like that happens *and* you're ducking my calls? Nah, that wasn't going to work.

I posted up outside of my cousin's girl's house with one of my people for days, and when he finally showed, I ran straight up on him and put my pistol in his face, like, "Yo, what's up? You got my money or what?"

He started pleading the Fifth, talking about: "I don't know," "I had nothing to do with it," "It wasn't me," and all that.

Us being cousins and all, I don't think he understood just how serious I was. I was really ready to knock him off, but my man was like, "That's your cousin, bro. Think about the effect that will have on your family."

To be honest, at that moment I didn't care. It wasn't even about the money. Well, it *was*, but it was about way more than that, too. More than anything, it was about the principle. He'd taken advantage of my trust and I was down bad.

I could hear Marky Mark's voice in my head, too. *I don't take no shorts.* I felt like that should be especially true with kin. I couldn't believe family would put me in that position, and just thinking about it made my blood boil all over again.

Still, I held off, and we eventually let him go.

■ ■ ■

Things got real bad after that. Real, real bad. My dreams had been so big, too. Music was going to be my way out. Me and Kink were going to put the 'hood on the map. We were going to take over the world!

But as the losses piled up, I was struggling just to pay bills. I had to fall back. I downsized everything. I got rid of my secret spot in Atlanta, broke the lease on my fly-ass condo in the Mack, and started selling my cars. I even broke the seal on the money I had stashed in people's attics and yards all over the state. It was deep. It was so deep, at one point I was living in the studio because I didn't have anywhere else to go, sleeping on that little-ass couch with two pistols on me in case anyone tried to come through the door.

Even then, I could literally barely keep the lights on. I'd walk in and hit the switch and it'd just be all that equipment, that little gray couch and me with my two pistols sitting in the dark like, *Damn.*

I went back to selling ninas just to maintain and started thinking seriously about getting out of the game for good. I didn't know what else I would do if I did, but I just felt like, *Whatever this is, this isn't it. I'm way too stressed.*

Then one day I was kicking it at the studio with my partner, and he told me, "You might as well do it yourself."

I was like, "What, rap?"

He was like, "Yeah."

My first thought was, *I'm not a rapper, I'm a hustler.* But after he left, I kept thinking about that conversation. I didn't know a damn thing about rapping. I mean, I used to rap here and there in the school lunchrooms and all that, and when we were working with the group, I'd help them with some things where I could, but like I said, I never wanted to be a rapper. I just wanted to make it.

But then I thought, *What if what it takes for me to make it is for me to try to become a star?*

I pulled out a beat CD I'd gotten from an Atlanta producer I'd met named Pretty Ken. He was down with the Dungeon Family, which was OutKast and Goodie Mob's crew, but his beats were a little more street than what they typically had going on. When I'd first hollered at him, I'd been thinking it would be good to have some beats on deck for whenever we finally signed some new artists to Young Gunz. I certainly hadn't been thinking our new artist might be me.

I found a beat I liked and put it on loop. Then I grabbed one of the long yellow legal pads we always had lying around, picked up a pen, and started to write.

CHAPTER SEVEN

The Come Up

The first songs I ever wrote were trash. Straight up.

I'm not talking about those first songs I wrote that first night either. I'm talking about all the songs I wrote for years. Thousands and thousands of them, and every single one of them was trash.

Over time, I realized the quality of the songs wasn't the point. It was about the process. Until I picked up that pen that first night, I'd never written a song in my life, and I had a lot to learn. I had to get those reps in, just like with anything else. It was practice, fail, practice, fail, practice, fail—again and again and again.

I will say this, though: once I started writing, I saw how rewarding it was. I'd been so in my head and stressed, even writing bad songs was therapeutic. It was like journaling in a sense in that it gave me an outlet. Plus, since I was sleeping in the studio anyway, I just stayed at it, and slowly but surely I started to hone my craft.

Of course, if I could have written a whole bunch of hits right out the gate, that would have been great, but that's not how it went for me. I'm sure you've heard it before, but it's absolutely true: you can have all the talent in the world, but if you're not willing to put in the work, all of that talent is just going to go to waste.

For me, doing the work was never a problem. Once my mind is made up, I'm going all in. My discipline is unmatched. When it came to my music, the only real questions were: *Would all of that hard work pay off? And if so, when?*

The way I was living, I wasn't sure how much longer I had.

■ ■ ■

"There go Shawty Redd right there," one of the homies said, pointing across the room.

I looked and sure enough there he was, right in the middle of the dance floor. Skinny dude, light-skinned, and from the looks of it, about to fight. He was facing off with this other cat and they were mean-mugging so hard, I remember thinking, *Oh, shit, this dude Shawty Redd is wild! It's about to go off!*

The DJ dropped the next song and I realized I'd had it all wrong. Shawty and dude weren't about to fight, they were having a dance-off. I'd never seen anything like it.

That's one thing I quickly learned about Shawty Redd: in addition to being one of the dopest producers I've ever known, he can dance like a motherfucker. Matter of fact, a lot of the big dance crazes that broke out of Atlanta back in the early 2000s—like the whole snap music wave and all that—started right there in that same club, The Bounce, over on the west side. And a lot of them started with him.

I'd gone looking for Shawty that night because he'd done a song with this cat named Drama (not the DJ) that was taking over the city. The song was "Left, Right, Left" and it had an edge to it that you didn't really hear in a lot of the other big records coming out of Atlanta at the time. This was late 1999, early 2000, and "Left,

Right, Left" along with Pastor Troy's "No Mo Play in G.A." signaled a shift.

Back then, Atlanta was really more of an R&B scene. The big producers were Babyface, Dallas Austin, and Jermaine Dupri, and they were making hits—I'm talking *hits*—with acts like Whitney Houston, Toni Braxton, Jagged Edge, Usher, and TLC. And then on the rap side, you had the whole Dungeon Family movement with OutKast and Goodie Mob and them, and they were on some elevated, super artistic, intellectual space-age musical shit.

Don't get me wrong, all that music was dope, but "No Mo Play in G.A." and "Left, Right, Left" were *hard*. Not only that, but they sounded like the streets. As soon as I heard "Left, Right, Left" I thought, *I'm trying to make music like that!* That's when I went looking for Shawty Redd.

We chopped it up a bit that night at the club, and then whenever I was in the city after that, I'd pull up on him and Drama and we'd always kick it at this strip club on the east side called Jazzy T's. After a while, me and Shawty started kicking it outside of the club, too. We'd hit the mall, grab something to eat, whatever. Then he started having me over to the crib, and I'd come through and post up in the basement studio he had over there and just watch him work.

I was still making all my money in the streets—and losing a lot of that money in music—but Shawty was already making a living off of his music. In that sense he was really ahead of his time. He was an early part of that second Atlanta wave, and by the time we linked up he already had a deal with Warner Bros. and knew all types of things about how the music business worked.

I learned so much from hanging around him that his basement ended up being like graduate school for me. Everything from basic terminology to the ins and outs of music publishing to how to run a studio session and record—I learned all of it from Shawty Redd. He invited me into his life and into his home and taught me everything he knew. Even if we'd never made any music together, I'd love him forever off of that alone.

■ ■ ■

We'd been kicking it for a minute when I finally stepped to Shawty about getting some beats. He was in his kitchen fixing some food—that's another thing about Shawty Redd: he's a hell of a cook.

"Yo, so you know I've been working on my album, right?"

He was like, "I know you've been talking about it, yeah. What's up?"

"I was wondering how much you charged for beats."

"Shit, for you?" he said, throwing something in the oven. "I could probably do $750 each."

I must have had about nine grand on me that day. "All right, bet," I said. "I'll take ten."

From that point on, whenever I was in the city and felt like I had a little extra money to spend on some beats, I'd go spend it with him. I can't front, I know he ran the numbers up on me a little bit back then—but compared to what some of these other people were charging, $750 a beat was a steal. I swear a lot of cats were seeing dollar signs as soon as I walked through the door because they knew I was so desperate to get on. Pretty Ken, Pastor Troy, Lil' Flip—they all got me, and they know it, too, because I remind them of it every time I see them to this day. I was giving them *bags*.

The one who really got me, though, was Lil Jon. He was one of the hottest producers in the city at the time and well on his way to becoming one of the hottest producers in the game. Well, as it turned out, when Kink and I went to get a lawyer to help us set up our new label after everything with Young Gunz fell apart, we ended up working with this guy Vince Phillips who happened to be Lil Jon's lawyer as well. Vince put us in touch, and I gave Lil Jon a grocery bag full of twenties for one beat. There must have been $50,000 in there at least. The song was called "Haters" and I just knew that was going to be the one.

We put out my debut album in late summer 2001. I called it *Thuggin' Under the Influence*, which was a nod to two of my biggest influences, Trick Daddy and Tupac. For my rap name, I kept it simple and went with what everybody called me anyway—Lil' J. It was the first release on our new label, Corporate Thugz Entertainment, aka CTE, which felt like the right name for a fresh start. I've always believed in the power of words so I wanted us to put it out there. Young Gunz was who we were, but Corporate Thugz was who we were trying to be.

We pressed up something like 20,000 copies of that album and my cousins helped us with distribution. In the end, I think we sold maybe 500 copies total. And one of them was to me.

■ ■ ■

After *Thuggin' Under the Influence* bricked, I started losing faith all over again.

Money was still a major issue and getting worse by the day. September 11th had just happened, and the world was about to go to war. The global economy was fucked up. My personal economy was fucked up. The streets were a mess, and I felt trapped. Everybody, everywhere was on high alert, including me.

I was twenty-four and even though I'd had all of this so-called success in the streets, my money was so funny, I was still bouncing all over the state sleeping wherever I could: the studio, my grand-mother's house, at Kink's Aunt Sarah's spot in the Mack (shout-out to Aunt Sarah—she really held me down), or with some girl.

I was anxious and paranoid. I could barely sleep, and when I did, I was having the craziest nightmares because I knew any given moment could be my last. And all I ever wanted was to be free. Free from always looking over my shoulder, never knowing who I could trust. Free from all the homies dying and getting locked up and taking losses left and right, and constantly getting those phone calls, like, *You heard about what happened to so-and-so over such-and-such?* Free to love my family without worrying about someone trying to use that love as leverage over me, and free to just plan a Christmas with them for real because for a long, long time, I closed myself off to that kind of love.

Damn near every night, I'd wake up in a cold sweat and reach for my pistol with my heart pounding and my nerves shot thinking somebody had just kicked in the door. When I was sure I was alone, I'd put my gun down and pray, like, *Lord, please just send me a blessing. Please.*

Then Cuzzo called, and it sounded like he might have the answer to my prayers.

■ ■ ■

Now, you've got to understand, when Cuzzo set me up, he essentially left me for dead. I want to be really clear about that. On his word, I went to meet his people and I ended up giving *his* man a quarter million dollars of my money for ten dollars' worth of Sheetrock—if that bullshit was even worth that—and that one play fucked up my whole shit. Then, when I went to try to holler at him about it, he was ducking me so hard I had to hunt him down just to have a word with him, and he didn't have a word to say.

Things hadn't been right between us since, but when he called, I guess he felt like enough time had passed, or everything Auntie

Mother had been doing to try to smooth things out had worked and we were back cool, but I never let that shit go. So when he started talking about how he had wanted to pull up on me with a new play that could maybe make things all the way right, I felt like it was God answering my prayers.

"No question," I told him. "Come on down!"

I knew what I was going to do before we even got off the phone.

■ ■ ■

To be honest, I didn't think he'd even come. But sure enough, a couple of days later he hit me up, like, "I'm here."

Oh, shit, I thought. *Here we go.*

I had him come meet me in Macon in the parking lot of an Applebee's on Pio Nono Avenue that I used to use as an office of sorts. Mel Man's girl lived right behind the lot so it was almost like the same setup we used to have at Auntie Mother's house in the 'Ville, but leveled up.

When Cuzzo pulled up, he was like, "Look, cuz, I'm in a jam so I can't give you the bread I owe you outright, but these people I'm fucking with are fronting me some work. I'm thinking I can just leave it with you and you can do your thing, then I can come back in maybe like a week or something and we can keep it going and I can try to pay you back like that."

Basically, he was offering to be the unpaid middleman. He'd front me the work that his plug was fronting him, and as long as he got enough money back to cover his plug, the rest was mine. That's how he'd pay me back. That's what he was suggesting anyway.

I told him something like that might work. Then I asked him, "How much you got with you right now?"

He popped the trunk, and I swear he had double digits worth of those white squares right there in the car, and I ain't talking Sheetrock neither. These were the real deal.

I was like, "All right, bet. I got you."

As soon as he pulled off, I took them things straight to Mel Man's girl's house and stashed them in the attic. Then I hollered at my crew. I told them we were about to get some money, and of course everybody was hype.

"There's just one thing, though," I said, and that's when I started handing out all these big guns. I'm talking SKs, AKs, ARs. Everybody in the crew was looking at me like, *Yo, what the fuck?*

I told them straight up, "Look, we up and we're going to get it off for real, but if the people I got it from come down here looking for their money, we're not going to give it to them, you feel me? So mount up, because if they do try that shit, it's on."

In the end, it never even came to that.

When my cousin called to see about coming to Macon to collect, I told him somebody got me and I didn't have the bread.

His voice exploded through the phone like, "YO! WHAT?!"

"Yeah, cuz," I said, calm as hell. "I don't even really know what to tell you. You can come down here if you want, but I ain't got nothing for you for real."

I don't know if he saw it for what it was or what, but he never came. I don't blame him either. I had the whole city riding with me. I'm talking ten to fifteen neighborhoods, and everybody standing by my side was ready for war.

I was the big dog now, and the city was mine.

■ ■ ■

That's the only time I've ever taken anything from anybody in the streets.

If we're doing business, we're doing business, and I don't play about that. At the end of the day, all you've really got are your balls and your word and I've never wanted to lose either of them over a quick lick. I've also never really seen it work.

Everybody I've ever known in the streets who was really into taking things never seemed to be building anything stable long-term. It was always fast money coming in and running right back out the door, with the added stress of whoever's money it was in the first place coming back for it.

Yeah, I used to take things here and there when I was a kid, but after I hit the block for real and saw what it really took to get out there and get it—and the consequences that came with all of it—I cut all that petty shit out. Once I got a taste of what it meant to really work, grind, and hustle for your bread, I always wanted to make my money the right way, and I always felt like I valued it more because I knew what it took to get it.

But in that one instance with Cuzzo, I took it. It was the principle. He'd taken advantage of my trust and naïveté, and he needed to get a taste of his own medicine. The way I was looking at it, he had it coming one way or another from somebody so I figured he might as well get it from me.

At the same time, I really do believe God put that opportunity in front of me to give me a way out. I was down so bad and I was praying so hard that when the phone rang and my cousin was on the line talking about what he was talking about, I was like, *Oh, shit, this is it.* So even though it went against my code to take, in that instance I wasn't about to let it stand in my way.

Getting that call was a blessing, straight up, and it changed my life. After that, I was able to get back up on my feet and keep my image up while I pursued my music. If that call hadn't come through when it did and I hadn't done what I'd done, there would be no Jeezy.

That's why I thank God every day for all of it—the good and the bad. I know everything that has happened is His will, and I'm just here trying to be the best me I can be, learn the lessons He wants me to learn, get better, improve, evolve, and stay on His path. I know it might sound a little crazy, but that's what I choose to believe. And like I said at the beginning, you've gotta believe. For real.

PART TWO

CHAPTER EIGHT

The Greatest Show on Earth

met J-Bo first.

I was on my way into Magic City, which, if you don't know, is one of the most famous strip clubs in the world. Back then, it didn't hold the same place in the culture as it does today—partly because my career hadn't popped off yet, no lie—but it was definitely already one of the most important and influential strip clubs in Atlanta, and I'd been going there for years.

Magic City was another one of those second homes to me. Call it a home office. Whenever I was in the city, I'd pull up at Magic City to meet people, network, talk business, and do deals. After a while, it got to where the girls were just part of the decor.

I'd just handed my keys to the valet when J-Bo pulled up behind me in a brand-new forest green Sierra with the extended cab. I'd always had a thing for that truck, and I guess he clocked me checking out his ride because he leaned out the window and hollered at me like, "Yo, that's a nice watch!"

I was wearing a Franck Muller, flooded with diamonds. Of course I didn't know J-Bo at the time, so him just saying something immediately set me on edge. I didn't know if he was on some funny shit or trying to rob me or what, so I was just like, "Thanks, homie," and tried to keep it moving.

He stuck his arm out his window and flashed his wrist. "What do you think of mine?"

He had a cold-ass piece on, I had to give him that, and I told him as much, too. He hopped out the truck and looked at his watch like he was seeing it for the first time.

"Yeah, I guess it's all right," he said. "I've got a couple of other ones I like a little bit better, though. You drink champagne?"

Now when I say we went in there and that man bought out the bar, I'm talking he had them bring him case after case of Cristal, to the point where Magic City was running on E and J-Bo still wasn't done, talking about, "You better send them to the store!"

That's the type of shit he was on from day one. No matter how many bottles he popped or how much money he spent, J-Bo always wanted more.

■ ■ ■

A few weeks later, he hit me up, like, "Yo, I've got some people I want you to meet."

I pulled up on him at a car show on the west side that afternoon, and when I say the whole city was shining that day, I'm talking about it was one of those beautiful days that makes Atlanta one of the best cities in the world. Everybody had brought out all their old schools, all the crews were out, and all the girls were choosing.

I was in my work clothes, like always—black-on-black Dickies suit with some fresh white Air Force 1s—and when I got out of my car, this little kid hollered at me, like, "Yo, your strap's hanging out!"

I looked and sure enough, my pistol was falling out of my pocket.

"Thanks, lil' homie," I said, adjusting everything to make sure I was straight. The kid couldn't have been any more than eleven or twelve, but I could tell he had some street smarts about him so I asked him, "What's your name?"

He was like, "Peewee Roscoe."

"Okay, Peewee Roscoe," I said, looking him over. "I'm about to go link up with some people. Why don't you walk with me?"

That was the day we both met Big Meech, and whenever you saw Meech out after that, Peewee Roscoe was with him.

J-Bo was from St. Louis and everybody called him J-Bo because he was the junior boss. But Big Meech was from Detroit and Big Meech was *Big Meech* because he was the big boss.

Coming up, I'd always heard about how tight-knit Detroit people are, but I'd never experienced it firsthand until I started hanging out with Meech and his people. When I met them, Atlanta was pretty much every man for himself, but with them, it was the polar opposite. It wasn't about *me*, it was about *us*. They were all about loyalty, unity, and building a movement, and they saw themselves as way more than a crew. They were a brotherhood, and that mentality was right there in their name. They called themselves the Black Mafia Family and Big Meech had a grand vision for just how big BMF could be. He didn't just want to run the streets of Atlanta or St. Louis or Detroit. He wanted to run the world.

"We're gonna shine like new money," he'd say. "They ain't going to see us coming."

■ ■ ■

When I pulled up on them that day in the park, there were a lot of faces I recognized, but J-Bo was the only one I'd met. I'm not going to say too many names, but there was this one cat I'd seen on the block every now and then when I was dipping in and out of Atlanta's Old Fourth Ward doing my thug thing. His name was O-Dog, and after we all started hanging in the clubs together, it didn't take long for me and O-Dog to start kicking it on our own.

I don't care whether you're selling socks, rocks, or mixtapes, running a Fortune 500 company, or running the block—everybody's got somebody they like to hustle with, and that's who O-Dog was to me. We were sort of like Mitch and Ace from the movie *Paid in Full*. We weren't in competition, but we were playing the same game, so whenever we'd see how each other was living, it'd just be like, *Oh, shit I can do that.*

He'd get an apartment in a certain neighborhood, I'd get a condo. I'd tell him everything about my condo and then he'd get a penthouse. He'd tell me about his penthouse, and I'd start looking for a penthouse of my own. Just that type of shit. Motivation. Inspiration. Feeding off of each other's drive.

He had his crew and I had mine, but we'd switch it up. Like, some nights he'd be out with us, and other nights I'd be out with them, buying up the bar, throwing ones. We'd fuck up hundreds of thousands of dollars that way, every other day. I'm talking, one hundred thousand one night, two hundred thousand the next, two or three nights a week. And we'd split the bill. So if I was out with his crew, we'd get whatever they wanted and if the bill was $60,000, I'd throw him $30,000. And if we were out with my crew, and the bill was $80,000, he'd throw me $40,000. That's how we were rocking.

But that was later on. When I first met Meech and them, I just knew them by face from being around. I'd seen them out in the clubs, posted up, buying bottles and throwing all types of money around, and I'd heard some things here and there about how they were moving, but nothing solid. It was more so just rumblings from people asking questions about where their money was coming from, but that's how it always goes whenever anybody new shows up on the scene and starts flashing a whole lot of cash.

One thing about BMF—you always knew when they were in the building. It was the same thing that day in the park. The whole city was out in their old schools, but J-Bo and Meech and them had pulled up in those spaceships. I'm talking Lambos, Ferraris, and Bentleys and all that, and they were all wearing matching black tees. It was a look.

■ ■ ■

I hit it off with Meech from the jump. He wanted BMF to have its hands in everything—movies, business, fashion, publishing. Even politics. But his passion was music. Of course, music is my passion as well, and doing what I do, I've met a lot of people over the years who feel the same way about it as me. But I don't know if I've ever met anyone, anywhere, who loved music as much as Meech.

A few years before I met him, he'd launched his own label—BMF Entertainment—and whenever I'd see him, he was always listening to something. New shit, old shit, classic shit, one of his artists, what-ever. And as much as he loved music, he also loved to dance. I'm talking, I'd pull up on him first thing in the morning, and he'd be in the middle of the living room at one of his houses smoking and drinking with the music up loud as hell like it was a club.

I'd walk in and he'd yell out something like, "There's some food in the kitchen if you want!" And then he'd bust out some kind of A-Town stomp like he was Bone Crusher or something. "Help yourself!"

That was Meech. Always dancing, always smiling, and always looking out for everybody else. If J-Bo always wanted more, Meech never wanted the party to stop and with that combination, we had some epic, epic nights. I'm talking legendary, blockbuster movie-type shit, so much so that I could write a whole other book just about *that*, but to be honest I wouldn't even know where to start.

Like, there was Meech's thirty-fifth birthday party, right? That was a night. He had it over at Justin's, which was Puff's old restaurant in Buckhead and was one of the most upscale Black-owned restaurants in Atlanta at the time.

I'd only known Meech for a few months when I got that invite, and let me tell you, that was a hard ticket. Meaning, you couldn't just be anybody and roll up and expect to get into that room. That party was a hustler's convention.

I remember when I pulled up there must have been something like 15 to 20 million dollars' worth of cars out in the parking lot, maybe more. It was the latest model this, latest model that, and everything was souped up and tricked out with the tinted windows, custom paint jobs and rims, and all that.

As soon as I walked in, I could see it for what it was. Everybody in there was somebody in the streets. I'm talking big dogs, to the point where if you couldn't put something together in that room, I wouldn't know what to tell you except you should probably be in a different game.

"Yo, Puff! Come here! I've got somebody I want you to meet," Meech hollered at one point, and Puff walked over, looking just like Puff from the music videos and the magazine covers and the tabloids and all that. I mean, everyone knows Sean "Puffy" Combs, right? Of course, he didn't know me. To him, I was just another street guy in a room full of street guys who happened to know Meech. Funny enough, just like J-Bo, the first thing Puff noticed about me was my watch.

"Yo, you've got the same watch on as me!" Puff said, flashing his wrist, and sure enough, we were both wearing the big-faced Five Time Zone watch by Jacob & Co.

That watch was *the* watch at the time, and it was so hot and so well known that everyone just called it the "Jacob Watch." They cost a little under a hundred grand, depending on what you had done to them, and I had two.

Now, just a quick story about that. Jacob was Jacob Arabo, and he was one of the most famous jewelers in New York. Back then, he was doing everyone's chains. If you were on and popping, you went to Jacob's shop in the Diamond District to get right. Biggie, Busta, Nas, Fat Joe, Jay-Z—they all got pieces from Jacob the Jeweler. And when he started making watches in 2002, that became the thing. Everybody wanted a Jacob Watch, including me. Matter of fact, I wanted a Jacob Watch so bad that when I got the chance, I bought two—the white one I had on that night at Justin's and the rose-gold one I wore when I walked up into the Def Jam offices to do my deal.

They set me back eighty grand apiece, and when I bought them, Jacob told me, "If you ever need the money back, just come see me and I'll get it back for you."

Well, when the time came and I needed to get the money back because of a situation I ran into in Mississippi, Jacob was nowhere to be found. I don't remember if he was locked up for something at the time or what, but when I took those watches to my jeweler in Atlanta to see what he could give me for them, he offered me $3,500. And that's not $3,500 each, either. He said he could give me $3,500 for both. The lawyers told me I can't say what my jeweler said and did to explain to me why he thought that's what they were worth, but let's just say that when he showed me what he was talking about, I almost died. I couldn't believe it, and I was so disgusted by the whole situation that I took the $3,500 and left those watches right there on the counter, and I never went back to get them either.

As for Puff, I don't think he really realized I made music until much later on. For a long time, he just knew me as a street guy who was cool with Meech who could take him and his girl, Kim Porter, out, and we'd be good all over the city, even in the 'hood spots, and we'd never have any problems because everybody in the city knew how I was rocking.

■ ■ ■

One night, it was maybe about five or six in the morning, and I was at the studio when one of the homies hit me up.

"Yo, where you at? Dude wants to talk to you."

It was November 2003, and by that point I already knew *Dude* was Meech.

When Meech jumped on the line, he kept it quick. "Yo, come to the Couch."

The Couch was one of Meech's houses in Buckhead. He had a few of those scattered all over the city and they all had their own names. The code was simple—the White House was this big-ass white house, the Gate had a gate, and so on—but if you didn't know what you were looking for, you'd never know which house was his.

The Couch and the Kitchen were like Tony Montana trap houses, and they were literally two blocks away from each other in one of the city's most upscale neighborhoods. I'd always been doing my thing out of shotgun homes, but that wasn't Meech's style. He had mansions. I'm talking marble floors, stainless steel appliances, and all that. Where the Kitchen was completely empty, the Couch had a sofa in the living room and a couple of beds upstairs, so you know—*the Couch.*

The sun was just starting to break when I pulled up. I could tell by all the cars parked in the drive that something was up but I wasn't prepared to find Meech laid out on that one couch, with everybody in the building on code red, and blood all over the floor.

When I walked in, Meech hollered out, "Motherfucker shot me! Can you believe that shit? Shot me right in the ass!"

Of course, my mind was racing like *Who? What? When?* But there was no time for all that. We got Meech to the hospital and after we got him situated, the crew filled me in. Apparently some shit had popped off in the parking lot of this club, Chaos, and Meech wasn't the only one who'd gotten shot. Two other people, including one of Puff's old bodyguards, Anthony "Wolf" Jones, were dead.

■ ■ ■

As soon as I knew Meech was going to be okay, I started to get that feeling like, *It's time for me to go.* I didn't want to stick around long enough for people to show up and start asking questions. Before I bounced, I stopped by Meech's room to make sure he was straight, and I was glad to see he was in a much better mood.

"Man, can you believe this shit?" he said, with a grin. "Motherfucker shot me right in the ass."

That was Meech. No matter what was going on, he was always going to find a way to stay upbeat. Not even getting shot in the ass could mess with him for long. Hell, not even getting shot in the ass and then being charged with double homicide and put on house arrest while the case worked its way through the courts could keep him down.

Instead of sitting at home all day sulking about it, he rented out the presidential suite at the old Swissôtel during his work release "business hours" and brought the party to him. We'd pull up on him over there at something like six o'clock in the morning, and he'd have all the strippers come through after their shifts. Then he'd break out these big-ass Saran-Wrapped bricks of $50,000 in ones, and we'd spend the whole day treating that presidential suite like the club. That went on for months.

Like I said, though, that was Meech. He was like that in the face of *whatever*. Like when he bought that infamous THE WORLD IS BMF'S billboard in the spring of 2004 and put it where you couldn't miss it, just off I-75. With everything going on, I remember telling him, like, "Yo, bro, that's a lot. Just think about how all those prosecutors and police and all of them are going to feel driving past that every day."

Meech wasn't fazed. "Man, fuck that," he said. "Let them do their job."

He wasn't sweating any of it, and sometimes I felt like I was sweating too much. My default setting was always that things could go quickly from bad to worse to way, way worse, which is why I wasn't at Chaos that night in the first place and I was at the studio instead. Matter of fact, that's why I was always at the studio, at least as much as I could afford. I just had this feeling that the walls were closing in—that they were always closing in—and I was hustling as hard as I could to get out before we all ended up trapped.

CHAPTER NINE

Branding 101

The first major label meeting I ever took was with Shawty Redd. Technically, it was his meeting. I was just along for the ride.

This was the summer of 2001 or something like that, and Warner Bros. wanted Shawty to come out to LA so they could talk about the situation he had with them. When he hit me up and asked me if I wanted to go, I told him, "Hell yeah! Just let me know how much you need for the ticket. I'm in."

He was like, "Yo, you ain't gotta worry about the ticket, bro. The label will cover all that. All we've got to worry about is the food."

That blew my mind. I'd been paying my own way for so long, I thought that's how everybody was moving. Come to find out, I had that all wrong.

That trip was dope, and getting exposure to that side of the industry was invaluable to me. That was another one of those things Shawty did for me early on that he didn't have to do. He let me sit in on a couple of meetings and even played some of the executives a few of my songs.

By the time we were on the plane headed back to the A, I had a better sense of how those meetings went, what the executives were looking for in that type of setting, and what to expect walking in. I also had a better idea of what I might be looking for if and when I did a major deal. Coming back to Atlanta, I knew I didn't want to do a deal just to do a deal. I wanted to find a real partner. Even more than that, though, I wanted to build a movement.

■ ■ ■

For a minute there I actually thought I was about to become a Cash Money Millionaire, no lie. And I was hype as hell about it, too.

I'd been listening to Cash Money for years. The way it went for me, I started out listening to the Geto Boys, 8Ball & MJG, UGK, and all that. Then it was 'Pac, and I was all about 'Pac. Like, that was my guy. Still is, too. Then it was Master P and everything he had going on, and I'd be at the record store every Tuesday buying every No Limit release. Then it was nothing but Cash Money—the Hot Boys, Juvenile, the Big Tymers, and all that. And Trick Daddy, too—I definitely can't forget Trick.

But in the late 1990s, early 2000s, the Cash Money movement was it for me. I used to wear those records out. Like, the Big Tymers' "Get Your Roll On," man, what? Listen, that was my *shit*. I'd ride through the Mack in one of my Lexuses, Rolex shining, sitting on chrome, with "Get Your Roll On" blasting on repeat, straight bossed up. You couldn't tell me nothing!

Well, one night not too long after we got back from LA, I ran into this Chicago rapper named Gotti from the group Boo & Gotti in the parking lot of Club 112. I was pulling up in my 600 Benz and he was pulling out in his CLS500, and when he saw me, he leaned out the window and hollered at me like, "Yo, I'm about to go and meet Baby and them over at Patchwerk. You want to roll?"

Boo & Gotti had come up under R. Kelly and done a deal with Cash Money after they'd popped off on the "Fiesta (Remix)" with R. Kelly and Hov. They'd been down in Atlanta for a minute working on their album, and we'd gotten cool just kicking it in the clubs. Of course, the Baby Gotti was talking about was Bryan "Birdman" Williams, Cash Money's cofounder and co-CEO. He was also one half of the Big Tymers and one of the big inspirations for everything Kink and I were trying to do with CTE. What I'm saying is, Gotti didn't have to ask me twice.

"Bet," I told him. "I'll be right there."

I zoomed back up I-75 to Buckhead where I was living in a high-end condo under the name of this cat who played for the Atlanta Braves because I couldn't show that kind of income for myself at the time. I got fresh and swapped out my Benz for my Porsche, and when I pulled up at Patchwerk about an hour later, I cut the lights, checked myself in the rearview, and walked to the door.

Now, let me tell you something about Patchwerk: that place is magic. You wouldn't think there was much to it from the outside because it's sort of a small building and so in the cut that you'd drive right past it if you didn't know it was there. But as soon as you walk in you know it's a special place.

Patchwerk is one of the most legendary studios in a city that's known for making legendary music. It's the top of the top. Crème de la crème. I swear, you name damn near anybody who's ever made it in Black music over the past thirtysomething years, and they recorded some of their most classic records there. I'm talking OutKast, Goodie Mob, Lil Wayne, Jay-Z, Young Thug, Kendrick Lamar, Toni Braxton, Slick Rick, Nas, T.I., Scarface, Jamie Foxx, Rick Ross, Mariah Carey, Jagged Edge, John Legend—Patchwerk's got plaques from all of them on its walls. And that's not even the whole list! Like I said, *magic*.

"Yo, so I told them a little bit about you, but I didn't tell them you were looking for a deal or anything because I don't know what your situation is," Gotti said over his shoulder as he led me back into the studio past all of those plaques on the walls. "I figure I'll just introduce you and you can play it however you want to play it from there. Cool?"

I can't say I was nervous or anything because I'd spent my whole life bouncing in and out of all types of crazy situations in the streets, but I'd be lying if I said I didn't want things to go well. I fucked with Cash Money and getting down with them would be like a dream come true. On top of that, it would finally give me a way out.

"Cool," I said, and then he opened the door to the A Room and we walked in.

It was like stepping onto the set at *Rap City* or something like that with Mannie Fresh sitting at the mixing board cooking something up and Baby right next to him looking like he did on all the album covers and in the videos—crisp white tee, bald head, all tatted up with his mouth flooded with diamonds.

Gotti led me over to them. "Yo, Birdman, this is my guy Lil' J I was telling you about."

Baby leaned back in his chair and sized me up. "What's up, Lil' J?" he said, finally. "Where you from?"

"I'm from all over," I told him. And that's how I felt about it, too. I've had more than a few places that I've called home, but I've never felt like I had a "hometown."

"All over, huh?" he said. "You listen to the Big Tymers?"

I was like, "Man, what? Hell yeah."

They were in the middle of putting together the Big Tymers' *Hood Rich* album, and they played me some of the songs they were working on for that. Then, I played them some of the records I'd done for *Thuggin' Under the Influence*, and to be honest, I really felt like things were going great until I was in the middle of talking about one of my songs when the top row of my platinum grill came loose and fell right out my mouth.

I snatched it up and tried to play it off, but out of the corner of my eye I caught Baby giving Gotti that look like, *Who the fuck is this off-brand-ass dude?*

Needless to say, we never did a deal.

■ ■ ■

Before I got that bag off my cousin, I was putting so much of my money into my music—and losing so much money doing it, too—that I was cutting corners wherever I could.

At one point, I was even recording my music in a barn. I'm talking a *barn*-barn. It was at this white guy's place way out in Conyers, Georgia, which is like an hour east of East Atlanta. There weren't any animals still living in it or nothing like that, but it didn't have a bathroom or any kind of indoor plumbing going on, that's for damn sure. If you had to go, you had to use the one in his house. I remember being in there one night with Bone Crusher and when he said he had to go number two, that guy sent him to the gas station up the road. That spot was no frills for real.

After I got that bag, I leveled up across the board. Cars, clothes, chains, studios. Then, in early 2003, I started recording out of Dallas Austin's old studio, DARP.

Dallas Austin is one of the most legendary producers to ever come out of Atlanta. He had all types of monster hits, like Boyz II Men's "It's So Hard to Say Goodbye" and TLC's "Creep," and I'd gotten to know him a little bit over the years through my cousins and them because they all used to run in the same circles. And you already know DARP was nothing like that barn.

Everything in there was top notch. The mics, the mixing boards, the studio monitors, the *bathrooms*. The kitchen was always fully stocked and they'd keep these special scented candles burning so it smelled nice and fresh. It was a vibe.

Of course, that vibe didn't come cheap, but by then I wasn't pressed. Matter of fact, I was so comfortable with how much they were charging and I was up there so often that I developed a bit of a reputation for throwing money around. It got to where the staff would see me pull up and they'd start working the phones, calling people all over the city talking about, "Yo, that young cat with all those big chains and Lexuses is up here again."

Next thing you know, all these producers and artists and hangers-on would fall through trying to see what I was about and if they could maybe get a piece of my bread.

That's how I met Coach K.

■ ■ ■

Coach was still going by his government name back then—Kevin Lee. He was originally from Indianapolis, but he'd been moving around in Atlanta for a minute, and he'd already had some success. He'd been managing Pastor Troy when Troy first popped off, and had helped Troy land his deal with Universal. Coach was one of those people who used to come through DARP when the studio staff sent up the bat signal that Lil' J was in the building, and when I met him, he was looking for his next act.

I'd never had a manager. To be honest, at the time I didn't even know what a manager did. I'd been working with this guy Mike Dobson, and he'd been helping me out with a few things here and there. He'd book me for interviews and introduce me to people, that type of thing. Not that the press was banging down my door back then, but still, he had a couple of connections and he was doing what he could.

When Coach started coming around, Mike wasn't feeling him at all, and he used to always be in my ear, like, "Kevin's a vulture, man. He's just hanging around because he's trying to get some of your bread."

I honestly didn't really trust either of them all that much. You've got to think, even though I was trying to make it in music, for the most part I was still in the streets so anybody new who started coming around was suspect to me. But I could tell Kevin knew some things Mike didn't know, so I just played it close and watched to see how things would go.

That worked for me, but I can't say it really worked for them. On more than one occasion, I'd be in the booth and look out and see them getting into it in the control room. I don't think it ever came to blows—at least not that I saw—but in the end it got to be too much for Mike, and one night he came to me like, "I can't do this anymore, bro. I'm done."

I was like, "Damn, for real?"

"Yeah, I'm out," he said. "You guys do your thing. I wish you nothing but the best."

That was that. I can't say I was expecting it, really, but I already knew what it was. I do have to shout him out, though, because he never made a big thing about it, and when the time came, he respectfully walked away.

After that, it was me and Coach in the studio, night after night after night. And I'll say this about Coach—he never left. His day wasn't done until my day was done, so if I was in the studio, he was right there with me. And he was always down to work. Coach was one of the first people I was ever around who seemed to be as committed to my vision and my music as me, and that's how we really synced up.

I knew Coach wasn't exactly new to the streets—he'd had his leg shot up over something at some point and still walks with a limp. But I know for a fact that he'd never been around anybody who was moving like I was moving *and* making music. I don't care what anybody says, what they rap about, or who they claim to be—nobody from my era, and I mean *nobody*, was moving like me.

Usually, cats who are trying to rap will have somebody in their corner paying for it behind the scenes, but that was never the case with me. It was my money, my music, and my vision. And the more Coach learned about who I really was, the more he started to sound like Kink.

Like, one night we were at Magic City and some hating-ass motherfuckers went out in the parking lot, cut a hole in the soft top of Coach's partner's Mustang, and poured Gatorade all over his white leather seats. When I heard about it, I pulled that thing out and let it go right there in the club.

Pop-pop-pop-pop-pop-pop!

Whenever Coach saw things like that, he'd always be like, "Yo! You've got to put this shit in your music!"

That was Coach, always pushing me to do more. He'd have me in the studio for hours doing take after take after take, working on one song. It would get to the point where when I finally felt like I had it, I'd walk out of the booth and tell the engineer, "Yo, that's the one. Play it back."

And I swear, ten times out of ten, Coach would be like, "Nah, let's do it again."

Matter of fact, that's how he got his name. He was so relentless with it that he'd have me in the studio feeling like I was running laps. Just to fuck with him, I started being like, "Okay, Coach," and "Sure thing, Coach," and "All right, Coach, whatever you say."

From that point on, I just started calling him Coach K. It stuck, and he's been Coach K ever since.

■ ■ ■

At a certain point, I started to think I might need a new name as well. To be honest, I'd never really felt like "Lil' J" was it. It was cool, and it was true to me—I'd been Lil' J my whole life—but it almost felt a little too grounded, and I knew if I was ever really going to make it in music for real, I needed to be a star.

That was actually always a bit of a challenge for me because I've always been big on authenticity. In the streets your word is your bond so I never wanted to do anything to misrepresent who I was or to compromise my integrity just to sell some records. I'd never do that in any other aspect of my life, so why would I do it for music?

At the same time, I understood that music is entertainment and a big part of the business is the show. The fans want to invest in someone who seems larger than life. Coach and Kink were constantly telling me that my real life had that larger-than-life feel so that's what I should be giving the fans, but after a while I started to feel like putting my real life on all those songs *and* still going by Lil' J might be keeping it a little too real. The way things were going, my name was getting a little too hot in the streets. It was time for a change.

One day, I was riding down I-75 listening to the Big Tymers' *Hood Rich* when it hit me. Lil Wayne had been calling himself Lil Weezy and Weezy for years, and Coach used to always talk about how one of my biggest assets was my raspy voice, so I put two and two together and called Coach like, "Yo, I think I've got my name."

"Yeah? What is it?"

We'd been going back and forth about it for weeks, and he was anxious to hear what I had in mind.

"Young Jeezy," I told him.

"Yo, I love it," he said. "That's it."

I was that much closer to becoming a star.

■ ■ ■

I can't tell you when the first Young Jeezy album came out because it didn't have an exact date, but it was sometime in summer 2003. I called it *Come Shop Wit Me*, and I took a couple of the biggest songs from *Thuggin' Under the Influence*, and a bunch of other records I'd been working on and packaged them all together as a double disc.

We pressed up something like 20,000 units and I remember going to Turtle's Records & Tapes in the Greenbriar Mall and buying a copy for myself just to help with the overall sales. Of course, me buying that one copy didn't do much, and in the end we ended up giving a whole lot of copies of that album away for free.

Still, *Come Shop Wit Me* was another one of those important stepping stones. It didn't make as big of a splash as I might have hoped, but just going through the process of putting it together and getting it out there showed me a whole lot about how it was done.

By that time, the Atlanta rap scene was popping. T.I. and Bone Crusher were out there with the "Never Scared (Remix)," the YoungBloodZ were doing their thing with "Damn," Lil Jon was everywhere, and I was right in the middle of that mix. There was so much going on and so much attention on the city, I felt like if I could just catch that wave, I could make the transition from the streets into music for good. I knew it was possible because I was seeing it all around me, but I also knew that I hadn't hit my mark with *Come Shop Wit Me* and I was still perfecting my craft.

I could tell I was close to a breakthrough, though, and even though I was spending all types of money on features and beats and studio time, I could see it for what it was: an investment in my network, my music, myself, and my team. *Come Shop Wit Me* didn't work in terms of sales, but the work we did on that project is what really set me up for success.

Over the years, I've gotten to know a couple of guys out in Silicon Valley and they've got this idea that's real big out there—*fail fast, fail often*. That's how I felt about *Come Shop Wit Me*. As soon as we put it out, I was already thinking about how I could go harder on my next project and improve. That album wasn't perfect, but I knew I had to put it out in order to take the next step. Otherwise, I risked getting stuck overthinking things, trying to make sure everything was just right before it dropped, and who knew how long that would take?

I always tell people when you're feeling stressed out, lost, and overwhelmed, you're better off taking a small step in any direction rather than sitting there not doing anything because you're paralyzed by your insecurities, uncertainty, and fear. That's what I did when I started recording *Thuggin' Under the Influence* in that studio in Macon, and that's what I was still doing when we put out *Come Shop Wit Me*.

The truth is perfection is an impossible goal. It's good to shoot for, but at a certain point, you've just gotta let things go. That's especially true with creative projects. The power is in the doing. You never know how people will respond to your work until it's out in the world. Everything else is just projection and speculation. At the same time, it's helpful for you to get some distance, too, because once it's out there, it's easier to see it for what it is—good, bad, and ugly.

With *Come Shop Wit Me*, the good was that after all the work I'd been putting in, I had a solid foundation. The infrastructure was there. The bad was that the album didn't sell, so clearly I needed more fans. And the ugly was that the product wasn't all the way right.

I had the name and I was getting closer to establishing an identity, but I still didn't have a sound. And until I had all three of those things—my name, my sound, and my identity—working at the same time, I didn't have a brand. And just like with anything else, if I didn't have a strong brand, I was never going to sell.

CHAPTER TEN

A Star Is Born

I knew we were onto something as soon as we got "Hold Up" in the can.

I'd cooled off on working with Shawty Redd for a minute, but right around the time *Come Shop Wit Me* came out, we locked back in. For months, I went over to his house damn near every day. I'd pull up on him first thing in the morning, and we'd sit up in the kitchen and eat and shoot the shit or whatever, and then we'd go down to his basement and he'd start building a beat for me from scratch.

Compared to DARP, Shawty's setup was simple. He had all his beat-making equipment off to the side, and then some studio monitors, headphones, and a mic stand right there in the middle of the room, no booth. It worked for him, but it was hard for me to write right there in the room. Everything would be so loud and crisp, it felt like I was sitting on top of the music and I couldn't really think.

So I improvised. Instead of sitting next to him while he worked, I'd take a pen and a pad into the little bathroom he had off to the side and write in there. I could still hear the beat, but it sounded a little more muddy and muffled coming through the bathroom door, and something about that helped me feel the record a little more. I don't know if it was because it reminded me of listening to records coming out of cars riding down the block or what, but to me it just sounded a little more real.

Every now and then, I'd dip back out into the main room just to switch up the feel, and once I had something, I'd practice my lines in the bathroom mirror until I knew how I wanted to tackle the beat with my cadence and flow. And that's how I'd write—walking back and forth between the bathroom and the main room, soaking up the beat, practicing and polishing until I felt like I had it all dialed in. Then, I'd tell Shawty, "Yo, let's get it."

He'd power everything down until he had the basement as quiet as it would get, and then I'd put those headphones on and step up to the mic and do my thing. When I was done, he'd fire everything back up, and I'd return to the bathroom and listen through the door while he played it back so I could get that same feel. If I heard something I didn't like, we'd do it all over again.

But "Hold Up" felt like the turning point, and as soon as it was done, I went to see my guy Westside Blue to see if he was feeling it, too.

Every artist needs somebody in their circle who's got a great ear and isn't going to mince words when it comes to giving them an opinion on their music. Westside Blue was that guy for me. I knew whatever he thought, he would give it to me straight.

I met him in the parking lot of Big Oomp's Record Store over on the west side. I was riding around in my bucket that day, which was like my work car—another Pontiac Grand Prix—and when I pulled up on him, he hopped in and I cued up the song.

Shawty's beat came on sounding like some kind of spaghetti western crossed with a goddamn horror show. Then the bass boomed and rattled the whole car.

I said I came into this game, young and yay tall
Gold Mouth shot me a bill, caught my first eight ball . . .

Hold up, y'all boys better get it together, nigga
Watch how I get gangsta, fuck with me, Shawty

Nigga, I was focused, that's what it took to get that
Now I'm 14, working with half a block, fam
With them hoes, getting money, having twice the fun
And don't play with it, dog, we got twice the guns
And I was young, serving niggas that's twice my age
Getting it, riding hard, getting twice the pay

Older niggas, hating, dog, they don't want it with us
See us in the street, dog, they don't want it with us . . .

Blue shouted over the music, "Yo, this shit is *hard*!"

That gassed me up, and I went back to Shawty's crib and got right back to work. The very next song we did was "Over Here," and as soon as we had that in the can, I went right back to Big Oomp's to see Blue.

I wasn't looking for his feedback with that one, though. I was looking for his help.

"I'm trying to get Bun B on this one," I told him.

Bun B is one half of UGK, one of the most legendary rap groups of all time, and there was something about "Over Here" that made me feel like it would be perfect for Bun.

After Blue heard what I was working with, he thought about it for a second, and then he was like, "You know what? I think I might know somebody who knows him."

He called up his guy D Money right there from the car. "Yo, D, I'm here with my man Young Jeezy, and he wants to holler at you about something."

He handed me the phone and after I explained what was going on, D Money linked me with Bun and the next thing I knew I had the song back and Bun B was all over it. I'm talking, he'd done a verse, jumped on the hook, all of that. As soon as I heard it, I called Coach, and we went straight to Magic City to see what was what.

In Atlanta, your music's not going anywhere if you don't have the strip clubs behind you. That's where the culture starts and stops, and for the most part it's a pay-for-play type of situation. I'm not saying the DJs are for sale—matter of fact, most of the really good ones aren't, almost as a point of pride—but if you don't have the right relationships and you're not breaking any bread, trust me, your song's not going to fly. If your song goes off during prime time and it starts raining cash when all the best girls are on stage, you've got a hit. If not, just know you're either going to have to go deeper in your bag or rethink your approach. And you might end up having to do both.

By that point, I'd been throwing money in Magic City for so long I was in good with everybody up there, so when we pulled up that afternoon, I was feeling optimistic. I'd never called in a favor on one of my songs, and I just knew "Over Here" was going to work.

At the time, my guy DJ Nando was *the* Magic City DJ. I'd gotten to know him back when he was still working day shifts, but he'd graduated way beyond that. Magic City Mondays was one of the biggest parties in Atlanta and one of the most legendary regular parties the city has ever known. And back then, every Monday, DJ Nando was in the booth.

"You might have something," Nando said as the chorus faded out. We were standing in the Magic City parking lot next to this old, raggedy-ass cargo van we'd had wrapped with the *Come Shop Wit Me* album art and that Coach had been driving all over the city for months. "Let's give it a shot."

And you know what? It didn't work. It wasn't a brick exactly, but I was in Magic City the first couple of times Nando threw it on and the best I can say is that the reception was lukewarm, if that. And that's being kind.

The truth is my type of sound wasn't what was really popping in Atlanta at the time. Yeah, I had Bun B on the record, but "Over Here" wasn't as rowdy as what Lil Jon and them were doing with the whole crunk movement, I wasn't as lyrical as the stuff T.I. was kicking, and it wasn't as heady and spiritual-slash-political as everything OutKast, Goodie Mob, and the whole Dungeon Family had going on. "Over Here" was a whole other thing. Even though it was one of the most up-tempo records I'd ever done, it still had a different, darker vibe.

The thing is, I *loved* it. Like, that record was my shit! It was my tempo, my flow, and my vision come to life over a beat Shawty Redd had made for me in his basement in real time. I felt that record in my chest—listening through the bathroom door down in Shawty's house and in Magic City, even if no one else in there was really feeling it but me. It was so authentic, so real, so *Young Jeezy*, I felt like it just had to work. I honestly didn't know if I had it in me to go back to square one.

On top of that, I was confused by the Magic City response. When I played "Over Here" for Meech and J-Bo and all the other guys I knew in the streets, they all said the same thing as Westside Blue: "Yo, this shit is hard!"

■ ■ ■

A few weeks later, I decided to swing by Magic City one night on the humbug. I was on a solo mission—no Coach, no crew—and the parking lot was packed. It wasn't a Monday, but it was prime time.

I tossed my keys to the valet and as I made my way up the steps, I heard a faint, familiar bass line coming through the front door.

Hold up, I thought, *is that . . . ?*

I walked in and sure enough the girls were on stage shaking their ass, the money was in the air, Nando was shouting me out, and "Over Here" was going *off.*

We gettin' money over here,
What it do, pimpin'?
See y'all boys looking but y'all niggas ain't tippin'
Hold up, aye!
Yeah, there's something wrong with it
If money gone, nigga, be the fuck gone with it . . .

I took it all in. The crowd, the money, the girls, the skin.

This is what I envisioned when I made this song, I thought. *This is what a* Young Jeezy *record sounds like.*

■ ■ ■

"Yo, man, I see you everywhere!"

I was posted up outside the Park Tavern in the middle of Piedmont Park, leaning against my black 745, when Jazze Pha walked up and introduced himself. He started running down the names of some of the city's hottest clubs, like, "Kaya, 112, Magic City . . . And every time I see you out, you're popping bottles and spending money and I'm always thinking, *Man, what in the world does this cat* do?"

I laughed.

Coach had me doing a few little shows here and there, but they were for half-empty rooms and little block parties at the end of dirt roads. They brought in a little pocket change, but for the most part, I was still getting my money in the streets. But that was on a strictly need-to-know basis. Jazze Pha was one of the hottest producers in the city with a bunch of Top 40 hits to his name and he definitely didn't need to know *that*.

I did need him to know something else, though, so I told him, "Shit, I rap."

He raised his shades and gave me that look, like, *Yeah, right*.

I realized what I must have looked like in his eyes: black-on-black Dickies suit, iced-out neck and wrist, dope-boy swag. Even as the words "shit, I rap" came out of my mouth, it felt like I was trying to convince myself. But then my hustler's ambition kicked in.

"I actually just put out my second album, double disc," I told him. "Let me get your info, and I'll make sure it gets your way."

We exchanged numbers and I pulled up on him the very next day. I knew *Come Shop Wit Me* had its flaws, but I wasn't about to let any insecurities I might have had stand in my way. Just like I wasn't about to fall back and sit on Jazze Pha's number on some let-me-play-it-cool-type shit either.

I know people talk about not wanting to seem "thirsty" and all that, but the truth is, you either want it or you don't, so you're either going to put yourself out there or you're not. And trust me, if you just sit around and wait for opportunities to come your way, don't be surprised if you end up sitting around waiting for a long, long time.

Yeah, there was a chance Jazze would listen to *Come Shop Wit Me* and be like, *Yo, I don't know what to tell you, bro, but this ain't it*, or some shit like that, but what would that have cost me? A bruised ego? Shit, if that was the price I had to pay for a shot at success, sign me up. If there's something I'm trying to do, I'm willing to hear *no* ten thousand times if that's what it takes to get to *yes*.

As for Jazze Pha? He was impressed. I don't know if it was the records on *Come Shop Wit Me* so much as he could just tell that I was serious about my music. Then, when I told him I'd been doing everything on my own dime, that blew his mind. It didn't take long for us to click up and get to work.

■ ■ ■

In Atlanta, the music scene is sort of like Magic City—incredibly important and influential, but you'd be surprised by how small it really is once you get through the door. Before I linked up with Jazze Pha, I was on the outside looking in, but Jazze was already in there moving and shaking so as soon as we started making music together, suddenly I was in the room.

Jazze had two partners in his label, Sho'nuff Records: Russell "Block" Spencer and Henry "Noonie" Lee. Block was from Atlanta, and I'd gotten to know him a little bit through my cousins when I was young. Noonie was from Oakland, and he had a separate company called Noontime Music with a couple of guys he'd come up with in the Bay, including Chris Hicks, who went on to become the vice president of A&R Urban at Warner/Chappell in 2004 and then the executive vice president of Def Jam in 2009. Noonie had this whole Bay-Area-to-Atlanta music industry network going on, and one of the guys he knew was this cat, Shakir Stewart, who everybody called "Shake."

Shake was originally from Oakland, and he was a special dude. He just had that energy about him that you see a lot on cats from the Bay. Like, he was the type who'd walk in and immediately light up a room. He was funny, flashy, and cool, and he really knew music. He'd gotten his start as a party promoter at Morehouse in the nineties and flipped that into an internship working for L.A. Reid's music publishing company, HitCo. While he was there, he actually ended up signing Beyoncé before she became *Beyoncé*, and of course that's the kind of move that can make your career.

From HitCo, Shake became a consultant for the label L.A. Reid used to have with Babyface—LaFace. And after he got to LaFace, Shake helped Noonie, Jazze, and them get a young singer they were working with at Sho'nuff named Ciara set up with Clive Davis and Arista through L.A. Reid and LaFace.

Like I said, Shake *knew* music. That's just who he was. Young and hungry with his ears open and his finger on the pulse, running all over the city and the country making plays. Of course, it didn't take long for him to become *that* dude, and when L.A. left Arista to become the chairman and CEO of Island Def Jam in February 2004, he brought Shake with him and made him vice president of A&R.

So, boom. Now you see the play. With Sho'nuff's connections and my work ethic, it didn't take long for us to put some songs together and start shopping for a deal. Noonie gave a copy of my demo to Shake, Shake took it to L.A. Reid, and L.A. told him to get a meeting on the books. A couple of days later, Jazze, Noonie, and I were headed to New York.

■ ■ ■

It was a bright, spring day when we pulled up outside of the old Def Jam building on the west side of Midtown Manhattan. They had this little circular drive back there just off Forty-Ninth Street and Eighth Avenue, and I hopped out of the back of our black SUV, looking dope-boy fresh down to my socks—crisp black Dickies, crisp white tee, fresh-out-the-box Air Force 1s with some iced-out rose-gold chains and the rose-gold Jacob Watch to match. I'd come to New York to put the whole industry on notice. I was a down-South hustler in the flesh, and I was ready to sell.

The Def Jam offices were on the twenty-eighth floor, and as we rode the elevator up I kept picturing how I wanted the meeting with L.A. Reid to go. I was thinking through everything I was going to say, everything I was going to do, the songs I would play, and the order I'd play them in, how I wanted L.A. to react to each song and how, by the time I left that day, I'd have a deal on the table, ready to sign.

I always do that type of visualization whenever I'm walking into a situation where there's something I'm really trying to do in play. The way I see it, if you can hold an idea in your mind, then you can hold it in your hand. If I can start to see the outcomes I want to take place before they happen, I know they're that much closer to coming true.

As the elevator kept climbing, I pictured myself in a big-ass conference room high above the city, surrounded by skyscrapers, sitting at a long table playing my music for L.A. Reid. I saw him getting hype. I saw me getting hype. And then I saw us closing a deal.

The elevator doors opened onto the Def Jam lobby.

"Young Jeezy?" one of L.A.'s assistants said, as I stepped off the elevator. "Follow me."

As she led us through the offices I tried to stay focused as I took it all in. This was *Def Jam*. Home to DMX, Ja Rule, Redman, Method Man, LL Cool J back in the day, and, at least until he'd retired at the end of 2003, one of my favorite rappers of all time—Jay-Z.

If I play my cards right, I thought, *Def Jam could be home to* me.

I went back to my vision. Executive conference room. Floor-to-ceiling windows. Skyscrapers. L.A. Reid loving my music. That top-of-the-world feeling. Success.

"Here you go, gentlemen," L.A.'s assistant said, leading us into the tiniest room.

L.A. Reid stood up from behind a desk.

"Fellas! Thanks for coming in," he said. He looked like a million bucks stashed in a broom closet with his fresh-cut baldie and designer suit. "Apologies for the temporary office. They're still building out the executive suite."

There were a few other A&Rs and executives already in the room, but other than Shake everybody was new to me.

"So, Young Jeezy," L.A. said as he sat down and leaned back in his chair. "You got some music we can hear?"

Aw shit, I thought, *here we go.*

For the next half hour or so, I turned my charisma all the way up. Now, I didn't go all the way in and jump up on L.A.'s desk or anything like that, but I definitely didn't hold anything back. I rapped along to my songs, did intros and outros setting the records up and breaking them down, and talked that talk.

I started to get the sense that things were going well when all these other executives started filing in. I don't know if L.A. hit some kind of all-hands-on-deck button or what, but as the crowd grew, I just got more and more hype.

As the last lines of one of the songs I'd done with Jazze faded out . . .

. . . And Jeezy what the rap game needed
Young, rich, thug nigga, and yeah, I'm conceited
And I'm nothing like them other guys
I'm the shit, bitch, you can't tell me otherwise . . .

I said, "Yo, so this next song is called 'Over Here,' and every time it comes on in the club, all you see is gold bottles in the air."

L.A. leaned forward in his chair. "Hold up, gold bottles? You mean like Cristal?"

"Yeah," I said, not knowing what he was getting at. Ace of Spades wasn't out yet, so what other gold bottles could there be?

L.A. was like, "You're saying everybody's got gold bottles in the clubs you're at?"

Now I was really confused. "I mean, yeah, why? What's up?"

L.A. didn't say anything and just leaned back in his chair. I could tell by the look on his face that that's when he understood what was really going on. I wasn't putting on an act or doing a whole bunch of bragging and boasting just because it sounded good in a song. I was who I said I was. And I was in his office, playing those records, looking for a shot.

For the rest of the meeting, L.A. played it cool. I don't know if he was weighing the risks versus the rewards, or just soaking up the music or what, but he didn't say much until after I'd played my last song. Then he leaned forward, looked me right in the eyes and said straight up, "Young Jeezy, whatever you were doing before you came in here today, you don't have to do it anymore. We've got you from here."

■ ■ ■

A few weeks later, I was back in Atlanta kicking it with O-Dog. He was showing me around the house he'd just bought with his girl, and he was big flexin'.

When he'd hit me up and told me they were buying a house together, my first reaction was, "You're buying a *what*?" But that's what they'd done—went and bought a big-ass house in her name. That shit was crazy. I'd never seen him so happy and even though I felt like it was a little reckless to rush out and buy a house with a woman he barely knew, I was happy for him.

But as up as he was, I was in a different place. I was relieved that the Def Jam deal was on the table, but I wasn't all the way right with it, and as we walked into like the sixth bedroom or some shit, I started telling O-Dog about everything that had been going on.

"So you're saying all this rap shit is really about to pay off, huh?" He showed me another closet that might have been bigger than L.A.'s temporary office.

"It looks like it, yeah."

"That's what's up," he said, but then he must have picked up on my vibe because he doubled back like, "Right?"

"Yeah, no, it's dope for real," I told him. "There's just one thing, though. They want to do the deal through Sho'nuff since Jazze and them brought me up there, but I don't think I want to do it like that."

"Nah?"

"Not really, nah. I ain't really feeling that for real. I'm a boss myself. What do I look like coming in the game coming up under somebody else?"

"Shit, so don't do it then," he said, like it was an open-and-shut case.

"Hold up, you're saying don't do the Def Jam deal?"

He was like, "Nah. I mean, yeah, if you don't want to do the Def Jam deal don't do that either, but I meant with Jazze and them. Just tell them you want to do the deal on your own."

I wasn't so sure. "You think they'd go for that?"

O-Dog was like, "I mean, what other choice do they have? If you don't want to do the deal, you don't want to do the deal. Seems pretty simple to me."

I knew he was right as soon as he said it. The only reason I'd even made it that far was because I'd always trusted my gut. At the time, the Def Jam deal felt like such a big opportunity for me to finally secure something outside of the streets that I don't think I was able to see it clearly for what it was: a deal. And just like any other deal, those same rules I'd learned back on Poplar Street still applied—my price is my price, and I've got to know my worth.

I went upstairs and called Jazze from one of the balconies over-looking O-Dog's big-ass new backyard. I can't lie, Jazze was pretty tight when I told him I wanted to do the deal on my own, but after I got with Noonie, we worked it out. And Noonie's such a G, his whole thing was, "Look, it's whatever. Just take care of us. It's all good."

So that's what I did. I bossed up and took care of them out of my own pocket and we went our separate ways.

That was one of the first experiences I ever had negotiating in what you might call a corporate setting. In the streets, there's usually not a whole lot of wiggle room. For the most part, there's very little give. *My price is my price* is typically the law of the land and if you cross that law, it might cost you your life.

But legal business is different. For one, the stakes usually aren't that high. And then, two, there's a whole lot more give because of the way legal businesses tend to operate—with fixed costs and variable expenses and all that. And it's that space, between the overhead and operating costs and the profit margins, that leaves the door open for productive negotiating and the possibility that everyone at the table can walk away feeling like they got a favorable deal. That's why I've always believed if you're in that type of setting and there's something you really want to do, you've just got to find a way to get to the *yes*.

In that situation with Jazze and them, for example, outside of the time we put in together and the studio hours and all that, there weren't really any fixed costs. It was just about coming to an understanding and finding the right number so nobody felt like they were getting screwed. That's how we got to the *yes*.

They were cool, I was cool, and in the end, I did the Def Jam deal on my own. And everybody got paid.

CHAPTER ELEVEN

Def Jam's Bad Boy

After spending six months on house arrest with everybody running around hollering about FREE BIG MEECH, Big Meech was finally free.

One day he hit me up out the blue. "Yo, we're going to Cancun."

I was like, "Who's going to Cancun, Meech?"

"We," he said, like that explained it.

"Man, who's *we*?"

"We, man, *we*! Everybody. Call everybody you know. I'm calling everybody I know. I'm getting a plane."

That was too much for me. "What you mean you're *getting a plane*?"

With his music blaring in the background, he was like, "What you mean, what do I mean? A plane, homie. A *plane*. And I'm not talking about no little G5 neither. I'm talking about a 747 or some shit, like those joints Delta flies. Depends on how many people we can get. Make some calls and let me know."

Sure enough, Big Meech chartered a big-ass plane and he flew everybody to Cancun. And I'm talking *everybody*. There must have been two hundred people on board, but it felt like the whole city was there. It was Lil Jon, Bone Crusher, Juvenile, me, damn near every stripper in Atlanta, plus J-Bo, O-Dog, and the whole crew. Meech had the flight attendants pouring Cristal the whole flight, and he kept dancing in the aisle and running up on the pilots in the cockpit talking about, "Yo, let me fly! Let me fly! I paid for this motherfucker—let me fly the plane!"

I remember the pilots hopped on the PA system, like, "Ladies and gentlemen, if you don't take your seats, we'll be forced to turn around and return to America."

It was wild. We did make it to Mexico, though. And we had a ball.

From the moment we touched down, Meech paid for everything. He bought out a hotel right on the beach and put everybody up, chartered boats, rented Jet Skis. I remember at one point, O-Dog was zipping off through the waves talking about, "I'm going to Cuba!" It was that type of trip.

Every night we'd all link up and mob over to this club called The City, rolling two hundred deep. That was the first time I'd ever been to a DJ S&S party, and I swear he played Fat Joe's "Lean Back" so many times. The song had just come out, and he'd play it a hundred times, and then throw something else on real quick like Usher's "Confessions" just to mess with the crowd, and then he'd be right back on "Lean Back." I'd never heard anybody break a record like that, but it worked, and "Lean Back" became the theme song of the whole trip.

That's honestly one of the best trips I've ever been on, and I wrote "That's How Ya Feel" on the plane ride home.

■ ■ ■

Meech and J-Bo were two of my biggest fans early on, and Meech was always a big believer in my music. Whenever we'd be out, he was always calling people over to introduce them to me.

It didn't matter where we were—Justin's, Magic City, any of the clubs we used to always be at in Miami, wherever—Meech was always like, "Yo, Puff!" or "Yo, T.I.!" or "Yo, Fabolous, come over here! I've got somebody I want you to meet!"

Meech and I have been through a lot—together and separately, good and bad—but I'll always have love for him for that. He always looked out and he always believed. And he always held me up and championed my music. That's one of the reasons he's a legend. Not for what he did for me specifically, but for what he did for all the people around him. Underneath it all, Dude is a good, solid dude.

But that's how I met Fabolous—Meech called him over one of those nights when we were all at Magic City, making a movie.

■ ■ ■

Not too long after I met him, Fab and I were both on set for Bleu DaVinci's "We Still Here" video shoot. Bleu was from California, and he was BMF Entertainment's flagship artist. When I was first getting to know the crew, Bleu would always hit me up to hang out, and since his album was going to be BMF's first big release, they were going all out.

The "We Still Here" video shoot must have cost a half a ticket alone, and that's strictly independent, with no major label backing them or none of that. They hired the director Benny Boom, shut down Northside Drive, and brought out all the cars. They even rented a helicopter. It was wild.

Fab had a verse on the song and he'd flown down for the shoot. At one point in between takes, we were chilling in one of the homie's Ferraris when he asked me if I wanted to hear some of his new music.

I was like, "Man, what? Hell yeah!"

Fab was from Brooklyn, and even though we were about the same age, he was already deep in the game. The first song he played was "Breathe," which blew me away from jump.

"Yo, this shit is *crazy*!" I shouted over Just Blaze's beat. "Can I get on this shit?"

Fab grinned, "Nah!"

Well, damn, I thought.

"I've got something else for you, though," he said. "I don't have it on me right now, but I can get it. What are you doing later on?"

That tripped me out, like, *Hold up, Fabolous has a song for* me?

I knew it was a reach when I'd asked to get on "Breathe," but that was one of those low-risk, high-reward, closed-mouths-don't-get-fed type of things. Fab was a certified star, and if he'd said yes, I would have been on "Breathe" and I just knew that song was going to go. But just asking about "Breathe" opened the door to the conversation about us working together on something else. That's not to say he wouldn't have brought it up on his own—maybe, maybe not, I can't say—but I'd taken the initiative, and it looked like it was about to pay off.

When he pulled up on me that night over at Patchwerk, I knew it was a big moment for me. A lot of guys can rap, but that doesn't mean they can sell records. Fab could do both, and I knew if I played my cards right, we just might fuck around and make a hit.

He cued up the song he wanted me to jump on, and as the beat blared over the speakers, my mind went to work. I could see why he'd thought of me. The beat was my tempo with some thick brassy horns that reminded me of some of the records I'd been doing with Shawty Redd. Fab had already laid his verse, but otherwise the song was a blank canvas, and as soon as I heard it, I knew I could get on there and do my thing.

He asked me if I thought I could put a hook on it, and once again I told him, "Hell yeah."

Back then, I was still writing everything by hand, so I grabbed a pen and a pad and I told my engineer to bring the beat back and put it on a loop. Then, I got comfortable—took my shoes off and everything—and I started to write.

When I felt like I knew what I wanted to say, I walked into the booth, pad in hand. I put the headphones on, looked out into the control room at Fab, my engineer, and a couple of other cats who were hanging around, and stepped up to the mic.

"Let's get it," I said, and my engineer let the beat go.

I got a pocket full of money and my wrist on froze
Fuck what you heard, we don't love them hoes
Aye!
Do the damn thang!
Oh!
Do the damn thang!
Yeah, a nigga might grin, but ain't shit funny
Got a pocket full of that do the damn thang money
Aye!
Do the damn thang!
Oh!
Do the damn thang!

But instead of stopping with the hook, I just kept going.

My phone is tapped, and so is my living room
We can't hide the money here, we need a bigger room . . .

When I walked out the booth, everybody in the studio was losing their minds, including Fab, like, "Yo, that shit is *crazy*!"

I hadn't put out any music of real note, but in that moment, I felt like a superstar.

■ ■ ■

Right around the time I did "Do the Damn Thang" with Fab, Puff started hitting me up about getting down with Bad Boy Records as part of a group. Actually, it was Kim Porter who approached me first.

I was riding around the city one day when she hit me up with Block on the line. Kim was always connecting people; that was one of her things, and she was like, "Block's got this idea for a group that I think you should hear."

Block laid out his vision. "I want to take some guys from the streets, put them all together, get everyone solo deals, and take over the world. I want it to be like a down-South N.W.A. Call the group something like . . . Boyz N Da Hood."

Kim jumped in. "Puff's interested in exploring the idea. Can you come by Jazze's studio tonight? We'd like to get you on a song."

After all those years striving and failing to make something happen in music, suddenly everything was happening all at once. Puff and them wanted me to get on a song? I had two words for them: "No question."

Jazze's studio was up in this north Atlanta suburb called Chamblee, and I used to always get a little nervous going up there because Chamblee-Tucker Road was a hot area for police. They were always pulling people over and setting up roadblocks. You know how that goes. Heaven forbid you get caught driving while Black or brown. A lot of times that's enough for probable cause right there.

Of course, most of the time I was riding dirty back then anyway, so I was always extra cautious when I made that trip. Like that night when I pulled up on them, I must have had something like $1.5 million in the trunk.

The studio was jumping when I walked in. Ciara was in the back with Jazze working on her debut. Noonie and Block were there, of course, and Trick Daddy was in the building. Trick was in and out of Jazze's spot a lot back then, which was always wild to me because I'd been such a big fan of his for years. Crazy enough, my first feature on a major label album ended up being on Trick Daddy's *Thug Matrimony: Married to the Streets*. Imagine that.

Block had handpicked three other artists he wanted to be in the group—Big Gee, Big Duke, and this young dude who could rap his ass off named Jody Breeze—and they were all over there, too. All in all, there must have been something like twenty or thirty people roaming around, and for the most part I'd never met any of them in my life.

Block did some introductions and then he cued up a beat. "I want y'all to write to this right here," he said, and then he let it ride.

That beat was hard, I'll give him that. The producer was this cat Nitti Beatz, who Block was cool with, and the beat had these crisp drums and a tight little synth line that almost sounded like some horns. Even though it had a little bit of a faster rhythm to it than what I was used to, it had that dark vibe that fit right in with what I'd come to think of as my sound.

It took Jody all of ten minutes to get down his verse and the hook, and it didn't take Duke much longer than that. The whole atmosphere was on some real rap shit with everybody in there going bar for bar trying to impress. Meanwhile, I was in the corner with my pad and pen still trying to get comfortable enough to write.

The truth is, I'd never worked like that. I was used to working in closed sessions, where it would just be me and Shawty or whatever producer I was working with or me and my engineer, Nico. Nico was dope and for years we were a dynamic duo. We'd make magic whenever we'd link up, but Nico wasn't there that night. Neither were Coach, Kink, or anybody else I was comfortable working around.

In the end, it must have taken me something like two hours to write my verse, and the whole time, people were just coming in and out of the room, watching and waiting on me. It was like I had a little rap peanut gallery in there, and after I got in the booth I could hear them making all these little comments to Block.

"Yo, what's up with your boy?"

"You really want this guy in the group? You're bugging."

"Yo, he can't rap!"

I'll be honest, it started to get to me a little bit, too. I knew I was green, and without Nico in there to back me up, I didn't even know what to say to the engineer to try to help him help me because I didn't know the right terminology for everything I wanted him to do.

I went back to what I knew—I put in the work. Just like I'd do with Coach, I started going over my verse again and again and again like I was running laps, partly because I like my vocals stacked so there's multiple takes sitting on top of each other and partly because I wanted to make sure I had it all the way right, to where I could feel every line in my chest.

It was a slow process, but it was my process. And when I finally felt like I had it how I wanted it, I walked out the booth feeling some combination of frustrated, embarrassed, proud, and relieved.

I told the engineer, "Yo, play that shit back," and then I walked out into the hall so I could hear how my verse sounded through the studio door because that was part of my process, too.

Meanwhile, all the cats who'd been talking all that shit started streaming in so they could hear the results. The engineer cranked it all the way up, and I came on right after Jody's first pass through the hook.

If it's taking too long to lock up, bring it back
You were short anyway, so bring a stack
"That shit was fucked up," I wouldn't even know
I ain't had to open up a whole thing since '94 (Damn!) . . .

I'll tell you what: standing in that little studio hallway, listening through the door, knowing I had that $1.5 million in my trunk, I felt that shit for real. As it turned out, I wasn't the only one either. When I walked back into the studio, everybody in that motherfucker was losing their damn minds, like, "Yo, that's gotta be the hardest verse *ever!*"

You're goddamn right. Everybody's process is different. Trust yours.

■ ■ ■

A few weeks later, I was riding down Peachtree listening to Hot 107.9 during the afternoon drive when I heard the DJ start talking up a song by this new group coming out of Atlanta—Boyz N Da Hood.

"It's called 'Dem Boyz,'" he said. "Hit me up and let me know what you think!"

I pulled over to the side of the road and there it was.

If it's taking too long to lock up, bring it back . . .

I couldn't believe it. I'd gone up to Chamblee on a whim and now I had a record on the city's biggest radio station in prime time. Not only that, but I was on the radio talking that *talk*. I wasn't the only one who was surprised.

"Damn, you really said *that?*" Meech said when he heard the song.

I had, and as soon as "Dem Boyz" hit the airwaves, it was in regular rotation and everybody was fiending for more Jeezy. Including Puff. Of course Puff's whole thing has always been *can't stop, won't stop*, right? Well, after "Dem Boyz" popped off, Puff didn't stop blowing me up.

One thing about Puff: he's a natural-born hustler for real. He's the type of cat who will hit the block and stand out there all night making plays and not even be doing it for the bread. He's in it for the rush. It doesn't matter what type of deal you're trying to do—big, small, whatever—if there's a deal to be done, he's trying to get it done. Doing business is a sport to him, and his energy is infectious. I swear, spend any time around him and you just start getting that feeling like, *Oh, I just know I'm about to get some money now. It's coming. Let's get it!*

Well, in 2004, the deal Puff really wanted to do was with me.

Whenever I'd see him out, that's all he wanted to talk about—doing a deal. And he had a plan, too. He wanted to partner with Block's label, Block Entertainment, to sign Boyz N Da Hood to Atlantic through the situation Puff had over there for Bad Boy South, and he really wanted me to be in the group.

Once he got that idea in his head, it was a full-court press. Day and night, night and day. He left voice mails, he had other people call me on his behalf—all of it. Puff was relentless. And every time it would come up, I'd always tell him the same thing: "Yo, my man, no offense and I really appreciate what you're talking about and everything, but I'm still focused on getting my own situation set up right now. I don't know if I really want to be a part of a group."

But he just kept at it. I'm talking to the point where one night he hit me as I was walking into Magic City like, "Yo, Jeezy, it's Puff. I've got the paperwork all drawn up. I need you on Bad Boy, baby. One signature and it's done. All you have to do is sign."

"All right, cool, look," I told him, "I just pulled up at Magic City so I can't really talk right now. Why don't you send over the contract, and I'll take a look when I can and hit you back?"

Puff being Puff, he was like, "Hold up, you're at Magic City? There's a Kinko's *right there*. How about I send you the contract and you can go over there and sign it and send it back and we can get this done tonight!"

I was like, "Man, what? I'm about to walk into Magic City. I ain't going to no damn Kinko's! Just send it over. I'll let you know this week."

I shook my head and laughed. That's another thing about Puff—24/7/365, he's always going to stay true to exactly who he is: Sean "Puffy" Combs.

That night, I sat in the back of Magic City lost in my own thoughts. The Def Jam deal was still in the works, but it wasn't done. And it wasn't like it was for a whole lot of bread, either. I mean it was cool, don't get me wrong, but the money wasn't the draw. There were so many things going on in the streets at the time—so many people dying and going to jail and getting stopped and raided and all that, that I probably would have taken half of what they'd offered me just to make that move. Okay, maybe not half, but still. I wasn't worried about the bread. I knew one way or another, the money would come. I was worried about finding a way out of the life I was in.

Still, the possibility of doing two deals was better than one, so as I sat in the back of Magic City watching everybody ball out, I kept going back and forth with it trying to figure it out. Could I really do a solo deal with Def Jam *and* a group deal with Bad Boy South/ Atlantic? Had anything like that ever been done? Would anyone even want to do a deal like that with me considering I hardly had any records sold to my name?

I didn't know, but by the time I walked out of Magic City that night, I was determined to find out.

CHAPTER TWELVE

Tha Streets Iz Watchin

One day in early 2004, Coach hit me up.

"Yo, we need to get you a show tape," he said.

I was like, "Cool. What's that?"

Come to find out, a show tape is basically a tape with all your instrumentals on it and maybe a few sound effects and drops thrown in—gunshots, someone hollering your name, sirens, and whatever else—all sequenced into a set so when you're just starting out and it's time to take your show on the road, you don't have to pay a DJ to go with you. You can just take your show tape and hand it to the venue's DJ. When it's time to hit the stage, all they've got to do is hit play.

Coach said he knew a guy who could hook it up. "He's cool. Lives around my way. Charges $100 a tape."

A couple of days later we pulled up in front of this tiny-ass house over on the east side in the Old Fourth Ward, not too far from where O-Dog and all his people were from. That part of Atlanta has gentrified a lot, but back then it was still pretty much the 'hood.

When Coach's guy answered the door, I swear the first thing out of his mouth was, "What's up, fellas? If you don't mind, just take your shoes off when you come in. You can leave them right there."

I know I gave Coach the craziest look, like, *Bro, is he serious?* I didn't want to disrespect the man's house, but I was living in a multimillion-dollar condo in one of the city's best neighborhoods. And some dude I didn't know wanted me to take my shoes off to step inside his *shack*?

I was ready to turn right around and leave, but then I saw Coach looking at me like, *Just go with it, it's cool,* so I slipped off my Air Force 1s and walked inside to see what this dude was all about.

His name was Tyree Simmons and he was a DJ's DJ. He had his records stacked everywhere and all his DJ equipment set up in the living room. And back in what used to be a laundry room or something like that, he'd put in this sort of makeshift studio just off the kitchen and he put all his tapes together back there.

Tyree was originally from Philadelphia, and even though he'd been in Atlanta for a minute, he still had that real true-school, hip-hop vibe. He was sort of crunchy with it, if you get me. Like, he was all about the craft, the wordplay, and the musicality of it all. Head wraps and incense and take your shoes off at the door. He was a college kid, basically, which makes sense because the whole reason he'd come to Atlanta in the first place was to go to school at Clark.

I didn't really know anything about the whole East Coast hip-hop scene outside of what I'd seen on *Rap City* and BET. I mean, I knew about it, but whereas Tyree was all about hip-hop culture—DJing and mixtapes and all that—my culture was the streets. Even though we were just about the same age and we both had a love for music, we were really coming from two different worlds.

His price was right, though, and the work was good. After Coach hooked us up, I started going to him for all my show tapes. And while I was running around the city and state, doing all of these little-ass shows for half-empty rooms, just trying to get my name out there, Tyree was doing his thing building his own name on the back of a bunch of mixtape series he was doing. He had an R&B series, a dancehall series, all of that. But it was this one series that he was doing that had a harder feel and was built around southern street music that really spoke to me.

There were a couple of other DJs in the city doing a similar type of thing back then, but there was something about Tyree's tapes that seemed to give him an edge. It was sort of like his secret sauce. Whatever it was, Tyree and his tapes cut through. He called himself DJ Drama, and that mixtape series I'm talking about? He called it Gangsta Grillz.

In 2022, Drama won a Grammy with Tyler, the Creator, for helping Tyler damn near turn his whole *Call Me If You Get Lost* album into a special edition of Gangsta Grillz, but when we first met, he was still just getting warmed up. Matter of fact, me and Coach went to the very first Gangsta Grillz event.

Up until then, there hadn't been a whole lot of fanfare when a new volume of Gangsta Grillz dropped, but that night they made it a moment. The party was at Vision, which was a club just down the road from Chaos, and it was packed. The music was popping and every so often you'd hear Lil Jon's voice ring out with the series' signature drop, like, "Gangsta Grizz-Illz!" Looking around the room, I was surprised to see a whole lot of faces I recognized from the streets.

At a certain point, I told Coach, "I need to do a mixtape with this kid!"

"Shit," he yelled back over the music, "let's do it!"

■ ■ ■

"Man, no disrespect, but I don't think that's going to work."

That's what Drama said when we linked up at one of my favorite sushi spots a couple of weeks later to talk about doing a tape.

The way he was looking at it, I was just another street cat with a little extra money to throw around chasing a dream, but that didn't make me a star. For the Gangsta Grillz brand to keep growing, he needed certified hitmakers—the more the better. That's how he was doing his marketing. Gangsta Grillz was buzzing because he was doing tapes with big names like Lil Jon. What was he going to get out of doing a tape with me?

"Bro, I don't know if you really understand just how big of a presence you have out in the streets," I told him while we ate. "I was at that party the other night and there were a whole lot of street dudes in there for real. They fuck with Gangsta Grillz, and they fuck with me. I'm telling you, we gotta do a tape. It'll work."

Drama wasn't convinced. Matter of fact, he was downright resistant. He was like, "I could see about maybe putting a song or two of yours on the next Gangsta Grillz, but doing a whole tape together? I don't know about all that."

But I had a vision, and I was determined to get to a *yes*.

I was like, "Look, to be honest with you, I don't even want to do a regular Gangsta Grillz. Don't get me wrong, what you've got going on is dope. That's why we're even having this conversation. But I don't want to just do a mixtape with you. I want to do something more like a street album. Call it a Gangsta Grillz special edition or something like that. I just want to work with you to introduce my music to the world."

I can't say I was the first one to come up with that idea—50 Cent and DJ Whoo Kid and them had used the mixtape-as-street-album model to really kickstart 50's career. And I can't even say for sure if they were the first to come up with it either, but after 50 got his Interscope deal, that became the blueprint. Instead of doing a demo tape, you did a mixtape and that's how you tried to get on.

At the time, my Def Jam deal still wasn't done, and I knew enough about doing business to know that nothing's ever done until the money's in your hand—and even then, you've still got to watch your back. Doing good business is all about leverage, so deal or no deal, having a hot tape in the streets would be good business for me. That's how I was looking at it anyway, and I spent the next hour and a half trying to get Drama to see it my way.

In the end, I was so relentless that by the time we left that sushi spot, we had a plan. I'd pay him a thousand dollars to do a special-edition Gangsta Grillz. He'd host it and help sequence the music and all of that, but I had to handle all the production, promotion, distribution costs, and logistics all on my own. I believe that was the first time he'd ever had anybody pay him to do a tape. Of course, a thousand dollars was pocket change to me, but I'd stepped up, invested in myself, my music, my vision, and my plan.

Like I keep saying—you've gotta believe. But at a certain point, there comes a time when you've gotta make everybody else around you believe, too.

■ ■ ■

The tape was called *G'z Up*.

I took some of the best songs me and Shawty had done like "Over Here," "Hold Up," and this other record I was really proud of that no one had heard called "Air Forces," put those with some of the songs I'd been doing out at Jazze Pha's, a few loose "freestyles," a couple of songs I'd done with Bleu DaVinci, and a few Jody Breeze records as a favor to Sho'nuff and Block, gave them to Dram and he went back in that little laundry-room-turned-studio and went to work.

Now one thing about Dram, he knows how to talk that shit— that's a big part of his secret sauce—and when I got the tape back a few weeks later and threw it on, he was going in. Right at the top of the tape, he's like, "Fuck that," all subdued and quiet-like, almost like he's talking to himself. "We gotta start this shit off right."

Then the beat to "Over Here" starts to build and Dram turns the energy all the way up.

Okay, you've now entered the Aphilliates chamber!
Corporate Thugs! Sho'nuff! Def Jam!
Fuck what you heard, Aphilliates represent the A-Town
If you don't know me, they call me Dramatic
My nigga Young Jeezy, Sho'nuff Records
Let's start it off right!

The beat drops.

We gettin' money over here, what it do pimpin' . . .

DJ Drama had delivered, that's for damn sure. Now I just had to do my thing and feed the streets, and I knew that wouldn't be a problem for me.

■ ■ ■

My plan was to drop the tape on June 19, 2004, the same day as Hot 107.9's ninth annual Birthday Bash. Now, if you don't know about Birthday Bash, it's basically one of the biggest rap concerts in the South every year, and it's been like that for years. New York's got Summer Jam, and Atlanta's got Birthday Bash. It's even bigger now, but back then, it was plenty big, too.

I knew going in that there would be 20,000 Atlanta rap fans all in one place, so the way I was looking at it, if I could get a copy of *G'z*

Up in every car pulling out of the lot at the end of the night, I might just fuck around and start a movement for my music.

But then, just as we were putting the finishing touches on everything, this young artist Lil Jon was working with named Lil Scrappy started talking up a movement of his own. He called it *G's Up*, and I realized unless I wanted those 20,000 fans to think I was somehow affiliated with him, I needed to change the name of my tape ASAP.

At the very last minute, we went in and swapped everything out—the artwork, the title, all of it. There wasn't enough time to get Dram to go back and re-record all his drops, so we just had to roll with that part of it as it was. The new name of the tape was *Tha Streets Iz Watchin*, and if you go back and listen to it, in one of the interludes you can hear Dram talking about, "Like I said, you are tuned into the *G'z Up* mixtape, the album before the album . . ."

What's that saying, though? Perfect is the enemy of the good? Yeah, well, the tape wasn't perfect, but it was good enough, and on June 19, 2004, while T.I. was on the Birthday Bash stage trying to do everything he could to destroy Lil' Flip's whole career, I was out in the parking lot of the HiFi Buys Amphitheatre with 20,000 copies of *Tha Streets Iz Watchin* on deck and a team of about fifty people ready to go to work.

■ ■ ■

Two nights later, Big Meech turned thirty-six. And that was the year he went all out.

The party was at Compound, which was one of the biggest clubs in the city at the time, and it was king-of-the-jungle themed—"Big Meech of the Jungle" was how the invites put it. The dress code was strictly camouflage, so much so that a few days before the event I got word that Meech wanted me to know that the dress code applied to me, too, like, "Tell Jeezy if he shows up in one of those Young Jeezy jerseys he's been wearing everywhere, he's not getting in."

Back then, those jerseys were my uniform. It was like a flip on my work clothes. I'd swapped out the black tees for all these YOUNG JEEZY basketball jerseys I'd had made so everywhere I went I was a walking billboard for my brand. Of course, I had a lot of love for Meech and I definitely wasn't trying to disrespect him on his day, but at the same time, *Tha Streets Iz Watchin* had just come out and I wanted the whole city to know my name.

So I went for the workaround. I hit up my man Tee from Exclusive Game and had him hook me up with a custom-made Desert Storm camouflage YOUNG JEEZY jersey just for the night, so when I pulled up at Compound, I was still doing me, but I was also up to code.

When I saw Meech, I was like, "You said camouflage!"

He just looked at me and laughed.

■ ■ ■

That was one of those nights that will live forever in the minds of everyone who was there. Everything about that party was big.

There was the eighteen-foot sign they had set up that spelled out his name—MEECH—in lights. There were the trash cans full of thousand-dollar bottles of Perrier-Jouët on ice all over the club, free for anyone to take. There were the girls throwing flowers at Meech's feet when he walked in on some *Coming to America* shit. And then there were the animals. I'm talking elephants, zebras, tigers, ostriches, monkeys, even a couple of lions—right there in the club.

There must have been two thousand people in there that night, having a ball, and that's not even counting all the street legends posted up in the wings. I'm talking *ghosts*. Like these were the cats you never see out because they don't even like to show their face like that, but they were all there that night for Meech. It was like the big wedding scene at the beginning of *The Godfather*, where everybody knows the feds are going to be running around in the parking lot taking pictures, but they still come out and show face out of respect for the don.

That was the night I fully realized exactly who Big Meech really was. I mean, I knew. But that was the night that I *knew*. And my music was the soundtrack to the whole event.

My Birthday Bash plan had worked. *Tha Streets Iz Watchin* had only been out for two days, but I swear everybody at that party already knew every song word for word.

At one point, I remember standing on stage in the middle of the club right next to Meech, J-Bo, O-Dog, Bleu DaVinci, and all the other cats in the crew, straight mobbing, with my music ringing off. Everybody was laughing and smiling, iced out and fresh as hell, with bottles of Perrier-Jouët in both hands. It really felt like we were brothers. Family. And as the DJ brought "Over Here" back again and again and again and the whole club kept reciting my words, for the first time I felt like I was actually, truly—*finally*—on my way.

CHAPTER THIRTEEN

Trap Star

One of the first things I did after *Tha Streets Iz Watchin* came out was take over the A Room at Patchwerk and make it my home.

The A Room at Patchwerk is dope. That's where I'd met Baby and them back in the day, and it's kind of its own separate section set off from the rest of the building. It's got its own separate entrance with its own gated parking lot so even though the rest of the studio is right there, back in the A Room you're sort of in the cut. Everything is real, real private. And then, because Patchwerk is right in the middle of Atlanta, it's a good central location that makes it easy for people from all over the city to fall through and meet up.

Once I had the A Room locked down, I felt like I was really ready to work. And in more ways than one, because I wasn't just making music, I was making street moves, too. I got real comfy in there, and I'd post up for days, shoes off, beats blasting, counting money, writing songs, and making plays. That was my trap. So much so, that I remember one time when T.I. stopped by and saw everything I had going on, he pulled me aside like, "Yo, bro, let me holler at you for a minute."

"Yeah, sure," I said. "What's up?"

I'd known Tip for maybe about a year and half at that point. Meech had introduced us one of those nights when we were all at Magic City, and I used to see him around the west side when I was in and out of the clubs kicking it with Shawty Redd. Tip was one of those natural-born entertainers. Charismatic, with firecracker energy and a crazy vocabulary. And he could rap his ass off, too.

When I met him, Tip was where I wanted to be—two albums deep with a brand-new, three-million-dollar deal at Atlantic for his own label, Grand Hustle Records. I can't remember exactly when it was that he pulled up on me that day at Patchwerk, but it was right around the time of his third album, *Urban Legend*, which gave him his first big crossover hit, "Bring Em Out." What I'm saying is, T.I. was a star.

I followed him out into the hallway, and he looked around to make sure we were alone.

"You know what," he said, with that signature drawl of his that anybody who's ever watched an episode of his reality show or listened to his music will know, "let's step into my office."

He led me into one of Patchwerk's bathrooms and shut the door. I had no idea what was going on, but I figured it had to be serious.

He checked the stall to make sure we were alone, and then he was like, "Yo, bro, you can't do both."

"What you mean?"

"The street shit and the rap shit," he said. "You really can't be doing both."

I thought about all the cash I'd had lying around the vocal booth when Tip had walked in. There must have been two million in there that day, easy, and that was a regular thing.

"Hold up," I said, "don't you?"

He looked me dead in the eye. "No."

I tried to blow off his concerns, like, "Man . . ."

But he was insistent, like, "Bro, you've got a lot of talent, and this music shit could really work out for you, but you can't be bringing all this street shit with you. I promise you it will trip you up."

Up until that point, I'd assumed that everybody was really doing what they said they were doing on their records. You rapped about being that dude, I figured you were *that dude*. I didn't think the culture would let you just get away with flagrantly lying all the time just to sell records. I mean, I had my doubts about certain artists and certain things they said, but after hearing the way Tip was talking, it made me think, like, *Hold up, you're saying this whole shit is a charade?*

That didn't sit right with me, especially because it went against everything I stood for. It was important to me that everything about how I represented myself was real. My word was—and is—my bond. There was—and is—a message in my music. I *am* the truth.

If I followed Tip's advice and quit the game but I kept making the same kind of music, what kind of example would that set? What kind of leader would I be? I definitely didn't think the streets would respect me if I went that route. I wasn't even sure if I'd respect me.

I didn't switch anything up after that conversation, and I just kept going how I'd been going. Camped out at Patchwerk, shoes off, beats blasting, making music, and making plays. But every once in a while, I'd hear Tip's voice in the back of my head—"You really can't be doing both"—and I'd wonder if maybe he was right.

■ ■ ■

As big as we were doing it in Atlanta, we were balling in Miami, too. Meech had his own club down on South Beach, Crobar, and I still had all my people in Fort Lauderdale from back in the day. To be honest, we were in and out of South Florida so much that it all kind of bleeds together, but there are a few nights that really stand out.

Like the night I met DJ Khaled, and he shot me a look I'll never forget, like, *Bro, who the fuck are* you?

We were at this club Amnesia on Collins Avenue, and it was set up sort of like a tennis stadium: big open room, no ceiling, with bleachers running up the sides so if you stood on those and looked out, you could see the whole club. Well, we were standing there doing it up, when I overheard J-Bo tell Meech, "Yo, there them people go right there. You don't see them?"

I didn't know if he was talking about some cats they were beefing with or what, but as soon as I heard that, I started ear hustling, like, *See who?* I wanted to make sure I was ready for whatever was about to come next.

"There go the captain right there," J-Bo said. "You see how they're all fake drinking?"

I followed his eye and sure enough, I saw a couple of cats standing around, fake drinking just like J-Bo said, looking like they didn't belong. Meech just brushed it off—he really didn't give a fuck—but I wasn't wired like that. I didn't know if they were the feds or the Miami PD or what. All I knew was that I was wearing one of my YOUNG JEEZY jerseys and my first thought was, *Damn, I picked the wrong day for this shit.*

At some point, I went looking for a bathroom and that's when I found this whole other room upstairs. It was like its own separate club, and it was *cracking*. Khaled was spinning, the music was popping, the girls were on point. I went back downstairs and told Meech, "Yo, there's a whole other club up there and it's jumping!"

Meech rallied the troops and we were rolling so deep that when we got up there, we took over the whole room. It was lit. There must have been something like three hundred people with us that night, and when Khaled saw Fabolous was one of them, he handed Fab the mic and Fab started performing right there in the middle of the club. The energy was crazy, and I was just itching to get on.

I tapped Fab between songs, like, "Yo, let me rock!"

But for whatever reason, Fab handed the mic back to Khaled so I started my campaign on him like, "Yo, give me the mic! Let me rock!"

Of course, I'd never met Khaled before in my life, and he didn't know anything about me or my music. To him, I was just another face in the crowd who happened to be standing next to Fab, and when he heard me hollering at him, he shot me the craziest look like, *Bro, I ain't giving you the mic.*

He did end up giving it back to Fab, though, and after Fab rocked a little bit more, he passed it to me. One of my guys slipped Khaled a copy of "Over Here," and I guess by that point he was just like, *Fuck it,* and when I say the room went up right after he threw it on, I'm talking we damn near tore the roof off of that motherfucker, mobbing to that song.

You've got to think, at that point, I'd never had any real radio play or none of that. *Tha Streets Iz Watchin* was still just getting out there, and Khaled didn't know me from Adam, but Atlanta was in the building that night and in Atlanta, "Over Here" was the *shit.* Halfway through my performance I looked over and caught Khaled giving me a different type of look. Instead of *Bro, I ain't giving you the* mic, it was *Yo! Who the fuck is* this?

That was another one of those early moments that really solidified who I was—in Khaled's eyes and in mine. Fab was already a star so for him to hand me the mic in that moment and for me to set it off, and in Miami—not in Atlanta—was huge. My movement was building, and to me, that said something about where I was headed and who I was about to become.

When I got up the next day, I looked out the window of my room at the Royal Palm and saw Bleu and all of them standing around next to our Ferraris, hollering at all the girls on Collins Avenue. Then I looked across the street, and on the roof of the building that was catty-corner to us, I saw a couple of black SUVs with some satellites on top. Then I saw some people standing next to those trucks with their binoculars out.

That's when I knew that the feds were watching for real.

■ ■ ■

I've always been paranoid. You could say I'm too paranoid, but to me, my paranoia has been a big part of how I've survived. I'm constantly thinking about what might happen next and what could go wrong, just trying to stay prepared so that I'm always ten steps ahead. I can't lie: it fucks with me sometimes, too. Over the years, it's fucked with me a lot.

It was real bad during that stretch from like 2003 to 2006. I'm talking *bad*. It got to where I was talking to Def Jam and Bad Boy about doing deals and *Tha Streets Iz Watchin* tape was taking off, but I just constantly had the feeling that the walls were closing in. I was out all night, drinking way too much, not eating right, barely drinking any water, and I'd come home to my condo in Buckhead and I'd just lie in bed with my mind racing. Couldn't sleep, couldn't relax. Then, whenever I did fall asleep, I'd have the worst nightmares. I'd wake up in a cold sweat, pillow all soaked, and I'd reach for my pistol, just knowing somebody had kicked in my door. And that was every day.

I'd get up, take a shower, throw on a fresh jersey or tee, grab my keys and my strap, and hit the door to go out and do it all over again, not knowing if I'd ever even make it back home. I knew my music had cracked open a window of opportunity, but I also knew it could slam shut at any time. So when *Tha Streets Iz Watchin* started to get a little momentum, I knew that was my moment. If I was ever really going to make it out, I had to go all in.

■ ■ ■

In early August, we were back in Miami for J-Bo's birthday, and we were rolling so deep that trip that we took over two hotels right there on the beach—the Sagamore and the Royal Palm. I'm talking there was nobody else at either of those properties that weekend but us. And we set the city on fire.

We were going so hard that Shake heard about it up in Atlanta or New York or wherever he was, and he hopped on the next thing smoking and pulled up on us while I was in the middle of shooting the video for "Over Here" at this strip club that used to be right there on the beach. I had everybody on set with me that night—Bun B, Lil Jon, Trick Daddy, Jazze Pha, Da Brat—and when Shake saw how I was doing it, with the whole building locked down and all these different locations blocked off, he was like, "Hold up, don't tell me you're shooting your own videos now, too?"

"You're damn right," I said, dapping him up. "And you better tell your people up at Def Jam to open that budget up, too, shit."

He stepped back and took it all in. "Charging it to the game, huh?"

I told him, "Man, what? I'm charging it to you! Y'all need to stop playing with me. I'm ready to go!"

He laughed. "I hear you, Young, I hear you."

"Yeah, well, you need to make sure your people hear me, too." Before he left, I made sure he understood what it was. I didn't need the label's money to get going, but I damn sure expected to collect every dollar I spent when I was done.

After we wrapped and all the gear was packed up and all the extras went home, me, Meech, J-Bo, Bleu, Jody Breeze, O-Dog, and a couple of other guys pulled all the cars into an empty lot behind one of the hotels and shot a stripped-down video for "Air Forces."

That was another one of those records I'd written in Shawty's basement, going back and forth, in and out of the bathroom, bringing it back and re-recording my vocals until I felt every line in my chest.

I went from old school Chevys to drop-top Porsches
You couldn't walk a mile off in my Air Forces
And you ain't seen what I've seen
I could get a 100,000 in these Sean John jeans . . .

Everybody already know, Jeezy a real street nigga
Every time you see me out, I'm with real street niggas
I hope you got yours, I keep mine
In the club, blowing dro, throwing gang signs
And you already know, dog
745 back-to-back, me and O-Dog
These other niggas is jokers
What they re-ing up with, I spent it all at Strokers
In one night, eight bitches, ten bottles of Cris
Forty grand spent just to make you glance at my wrist
Keep bread, so we carry them toasters
But keep back, though, my earring's ferocious
It's not just my imagination
I'm knowing I'm the topic of your conversations
The jack boys say they gon' rob
But on the real, fuck nigga, y'all don't want these
    problems . . .

There were no girls in that video, no singing or dancing or smiling, because there was nothing to smile about for real. It was just us, our cars, our ice, black tees, and black flags. As DJ Drama might say, it was just real quality street music—what they started calling trap music later on. In less than five years, half the people in that video would either be dead or in jail.

Now, let me just step back for a minute and say that when I was first coming out and all of this was going on, there was no such thing as "trap music," at least not how people talk about it now like it's its own separate genre and sound. T.I. had called his second album *Trap Muzik* in 2003, and that sort of put the idea and the phrase out there, but outside of what Tip was doing with that album, "trap music" wasn't really a thing.

That's not to take anything away from Tip either. He was at the forefront of a whole generation of street artists and wannabe street artists coming out of Atlanta and all over the South at that time, and what he was doing was real. Like I said, when I first met him, he was where I wanted to be. And he was creative and clever enough, and he had a big enough platform to where he was able to look out over the landscape and give everything that was bubbling up under him a name.

But I'll be honest, whenever I hear anybody start talking about the "trap music genre," it sounds crazy to me because nowadays it seems like calling something "trap music" is just a marketing term. It's a way somebody somewhere can package up an artist or an album or a sound, lump it in with all these other things, and try to sell their product to the world. But I know that all my people didn't die, or get locked up and go to prison, just so the industry could have a new genre of music to sell, you know?

If you ask me, there is no trap music—not like it is now—without me. I gave the world the blueprint. It was my struggle, my pain, my sound, my subject matter, and the way I was moving and how certi-fied and validated I was in the streets that really opened the door for all these other cats to walk in and tell their own stories the way they wanted to tell them, reach the people they needed to reach, and build themselves up in the music game. It all came off of the foundation that I laid.

I was the inspiration, and I know it because I saw it firsthand. As more and more people started coming to my shows and reciting my words, it wasn't just rap fans in those clubs—it was real gangsters and thugs, drug dealers, hustlers, and gangbangers. They're the ones who chose me and held me up, like, *This is our guy.* So while there were a lot of artists running around talking about the trap when I was first coming out, if you want to talk about trap music in that first generation—*my* generation—the way we think about it now, with the trap music sound and all that? That started with me. And even still, I think talking about "trap music" as a genre sounds corny as hell.

■ ■ ■

One day not too long after we got back from Miami, I was riding down Peachtree Ave., cutting through the city, when I saw a guy walking down the street in a Vote or Die! tee. At the time I wasn't really politically engaged. I'd never voted. I wasn't registered to vote. Nobody I even knew really voted like that because I guess we all felt like, *What's a politician ever done for me?* But I knew about the upcoming 2004 presidential election, that's for damn sure, because that's all anybody was talking about that fall. Bush vs. Kerry—that was the big thing. And I definitely knew about Vote or Die!

Vote or Die! was Puff's big Get Out the Vote campaign that year, and in the run-up to the election that campaign was everywhere. I'm talking billboards, posters, all on TV, even on the chest of some random dude walking down Peachtree. That's when it hit me. What if I flipped Puff's campaign and made it my own? I could call it . . . *Trap or Die.*

As soon as I had the concept, I pulled up on Shawty and we cooked something up right there on the spot. When we were done, I knew it just needed one more thing.

"Yo, this shit is crazy!" Bun B said, when he pulled up on me at Patchwerk to hear what I was working with. "You've gotta let me put a verse on this."

I told him straight up, "Yo, you read my mind."

As soon as I had Bun's verse locked in, I felt like I had another tape in me. I hit up DJ Drama and told him to come through. I had something he needed to hear.

Last time I checked, I was the man on these streets
They call me residue, I leave blow on these beats
Got diarrhea flow, man, I shit on niggas
Even when I'm constipated, I still shit on niggas
Let's get it!
I got some super friends in the Legion of Doom
They blowing purple shit that keep me high like the moon
I'm an affiliate, I know hitmen
I'm a hater like you, fuck my wrist then
Niggas sneak dissin' and that ain't how we play
Fuck with mine, get you Drama like the DJ
Now tell me I ain't real
This AR that I'm holding got a gangsta grill . . .

Drama was so hype he damn near shot through the roof. It was the first time anybody had ever shouted him out on record and as soon as he heard it, he was like, "Hold up, hold up! You gotta bring that back!"

I played it again and Dram gave me that face like, *I just stepped in some shit but damn it smells so good*. He shouted over the beat, "Yo, this shit is *hard*!"

Those five words were always music to my ears.

"This is the title track!" I shouted. "I want to do another tape!"

He smiled wide. "I'm with it, bro! Just say the word. Let's go!"

■ ■ ■

Dram has always talked his shit on tapes—like I said, that's a big part of his secret sauce—but back then, he was still building his personality up and building his brand.

This was before the *Dedication* series he did with Lil Wayne and Meek Mill's *Dreamchasers* and all the other classic tapes and series he went on to do. Don't get me wrong: Gangsta Grillz was bubbling, and he had some big tapes out there already, like T.I.'s *Down with the King*. But Gangsta Grillz wasn't *Gangsta Grillz* just yet, and DJ Drama wasn't "Mr. Thanksgiving," as he started calling himself later on because, as he puts it, "I make sure everybody eats!"

For the most part, he was still Tyree Simmons, an Atlanta-by-way-of-Philadelphia DJ, making some noise in the city off the tapes he was making out of a converted laundry room in the back of a shack in the Old Fourth Ward. So when he first sent me back the tape and I heard all the shit he was talking on the intros and interludes and all that, I gave him the Coach K treatment and told him to go back in and do it again. Then, when he sent it back, I told him to do it again. I knew we had something special with that tape, so we just kept going like that until I felt like every single word he said and the way he said it matched the energy of the whole project. When we were done, just hearing "Intro" gave me chills.

"Trap or Die! CTE! The Aphilliates," Dram shouted, kicking things off with his voice echoing over the beat. "Y'all niggas didn't believe us. We had a goal in mind: set the streets on fire. I think we accomplished that."

Then the beat dropped, and I came on spitting that gospel.

Here I stand, a grown-ass man
All by myself, a grown-ass man
A young nigga with some grown-ass plans
But don't point fingers, you don't know that man
You don't know his heart, you don't know his pain
You ain't looking through that scope, you don't know
    his aim
Minus all the videos, stickers, and flyers
Most of these rappers are compulsive liars . . .

■ ■ ■

"You're crazy!"

That's what the people up at Def Jam said when I told them I wanted to put out another tape. They weren't the only ones either.

"Dog, what the fuck is this?" Trick Daddy said one night when we were all kicking it over at Jazze Pha's studio right before Christmas 2004, talking shit and playing music.

"This is my new tape," I told him, cuing up another song. "I'm about to kill 'em with this one."

"Yo, you're tripping!" Jazze said. "These songs are . . ."

The beat dropped and he made that same face Drama had made when he first heard "Trap or Die."

"You need to be saving these songs for the album!"

I was like, "Man, what? My album's going to be way better than this!"

And I believed it, too. I'd been working on my album since before I even had the Def Jam deal, and I knew I had a certified classic in the can.

Trick sank back into the couch. "I don't know, yo," he said. "I know I definitely wouldn't give these songs away if I was you."

But I had a plan.

■ ■ ■

Going into *Trap or Die*, I told Drama straight up, "I'm not paying you for this one."

I'd come out of my own pocket and put 200,000 copies of *Tha Streets Iz Watchin* in the streets and now my name was buzzing. His was, too—maybe not just because of that tape, but it had played a part—so the way I was looking at it, he owed me one. But I wasn't looking for a handout either.

My plan was to treat the tape like it was an album and turn its release into an event. I was going to get a street team, put posters up all over the city, throw a big-ass release party, do interviews, whatever. The whole nine.

"I'll handle all that on my end," I told Dram. "I just need you to do the tape."

As far as I know, nobody had ever done the full-court press for a mixtape before, but that's exactly what we did. I put posters up all over the city and flyers in all the barbershops and beauty salons. I had spots running on the radio—all of it. I wanted everybody in the city to know that *Trap or Die* was coming on January 25, 2005.

That day, I stopped by Drama's crib to see how things were coming along and I found him sitting in his kitchen, stressed. He had his whole team in there with him, stuffing jewel cases, hustling to get everything out the door.

I was in a great mood.

"It's *Trap or Die* day, baby! Let's get it! How you feeling, Dram?"

He was like, "Man, like we should have gotten all this shit done last week."

"Nah, this is perfect. Look at all this magic happening in this kitchen! This is my element, baby." I pulled up a chair. "Give me some of those and watch me work."

I don't know if Drama ever relaxed that day—maybe after he got to Vision and stepped behind his turntables, but I don't know. As for me, I had a blast. We had the whole 'hood out that night—I'm talking all the 'hoods—and I balled out until like five, six in the morning. When I finally got home, I hit the pillow hard, and by the time I woke up, I was in a whole other place. *Trap or Die* was a sensation.

■ ■ ■

It happened so fast it was hard to comprehend.

One day, I was a street cat with a couple of hot songs on a mixtape, a few albums that nobody really cared about and a record deal—maybe two?—that wasn't doing all that much for me except putting me in a whole bunch of meetings where all these executives were always giving me grief, like, "We need something we can work at radio. Where's the single? We *need* a single."

The next, it felt like the whole world was screaming my name.

I remember being at the club a few days after *Trap or Die* came out, and all these cats were coming up to me talking about, "Yo, man, I just want to tell you that I really love your music." It was so unreal that I just assumed that somebody must have slipped them some money just to gas me up. But after it started happening every-where, all the time, I was like, *Hold up, this shit is for real*.

It was just so wild to me. I'd be in traffic and people would pull up on me, wave their *Trap or Die* CDs out the window, and holler my name like, "Jee-zy!"

The guys manning the old Atlanta tollbooths started waving me through, like, "You're good. Keep doing what you're doing!"

Even the ghetto superstars started showing me love, and that meant a lot because I knew how hard that love was to get. I'd been on that side of the game, so I know how when you're really in the streets, it's easy to see all this rap shit for what it really is—entertainment—because that's a big part of how you survive. In the streets, if you can't sniff out the real from the fake, you're done.

At the same time, when you're a ghetto superstar, you feel like you're a superstar already anyway so you're not really trying to be somebody's fan. It's one thing to appreciate their music; it's another to admire their movement and respect them as a man. But after *Trap or Die* came out, I was getting both—the respect and the love—and that was priceless to me.

Trap or Die became the soundtrack to the streets, and it defined that whole era. It wasn't just about the music either. We shot a docu-mentary to go with the tape, and in 2005 I didn't walk into a room where that DVD wasn't playing on loop. What I'm saying is, with *Trap or Die* we delivered the whole package, and it was an instant classic. That's not just me saying it, either. That's the whole world. After *Trap or Die* came out, everybody in the game was trying to make their own *Trap or Die*.

No other mixtape from the South had ever had that type of impact, and in a lot of ways it made Dram's and my careers. That's not to say DJ Drama wouldn't have gone on to have the same level of success he's had, but I don't think Gangsta Grillz would mean what it means to the culture today if we hadn't put out *Trap or Die* when we did.

And the same goes for me. I was going to figure it out some type of way regardless, but I don't know if I would have become *Young Jeezy* in quite the same way if I hadn't listened to my gut and blocked out all the voices telling me it would be a mistake to put out that tape.

Trap or Die changed the game and I could have walked away a legend off of that one tape alone. Even years later, those records still stand up as some of the hardest I've ever done. What's even crazier about the whole thing—I gave that tape away for free.

Dram ended up getting raided by the Atlanta PD for all the money the Recording Industry Association of America and some of the major labels said he was making off of mixtapes, but I was so new to the industry I didn't know anything about that part of the game. I wasn't even thinking about making money off that tape, either. At the time, I was way more concerned about earning my respect and putting my stamp on the game before somebody took me out or the feds locked me up. Even more than all that, though, I just wanted to be heard.

Like Dram says at the beginning of the tape. I had a goal in mind. And with *Trap or Die*, I think we accomplished it—and more.

CHAPTER FOURTEEN
Stay Strapped

When I first met Radric Davis, he was a Young Jeezy fan. It was the summer of 2004, and Coach had gone looking for this cat over on the east side who went by the name Gucci Mane. Gucci—or Radric, as I call him—had popped up on a couple of records and was getting a little buzz.

The way I was moving that summer, I wasn't really trying to make any new friends, but after months of blowing him off and him showing up at the studio to sit outside my sessions, literally bringing me gifts like customized T-shirts and rhinestone tennis shoes, which were a big thing back then, he caught me one day at Patchwerk when I was walking the halls.

"Yo, what's up, Jeezy, man?" he said when he saw me. "I've been thinking, and I've got this idea for this song." He started humming a hook. "All these girls excited, ooh, you know they like it, I'm so icy . . ."

By that point, I honestly felt so bad about how I'd been treating him, I told him, "Yo, you know what, bro? Fuck it. Let's do it right quick."

Now, anybody who knows anything about me and him already knows how this part of the story goes. At least the public part, that is.

When we got back to the A Room—and mind you, this is my session, my engineer, my dime—he started talking up this producer he'd been working with named Zaytoven, like, "Man, I'm telling you my boy, Zay, he's nice! He can play the keys, make beats. You've got to hear him. He can do it all. And he's quick, too. I'm telling you, if we get him in here, we're straight. I just know he's going to hook it up!"

Zaytoven came through, and even though his sound was a little more upbeat and lighthearted than what I typically had going on, he had a good thing going with Radric and it didn't take long for us to get something down. I hit up my man Boo from Boo & Gotti and had him pull up and do a verse, and then because I felt like it wasn't quite right, I hollered at this OG cat I knew from the Dungeon Family named Lil Will and had him stop by and redo the hook to give it that real old Atlanta feel. And that was it. "Icy" was done.

We were both so new to the game at the time that we didn't talk about paperwork or splits or none of that. Radric just took the tapes with him and left, and I didn't think anything about it—like the song wasn't even on my radar—until it started getting a little local radio play and all of a sudden all the Def Jam people stared blowing me up talking about how they wanted the song for my album, like, "You know that single we've been looking for? 'Icy' might be the one."

To be honest, I really wasn't feeling it. "Icy" never felt like a Young Jeezy record to me, so I deaded it and told the Def Jam people I had way better records on deck.

Meanwhile, me and him were both still in the streets—he was running with a robbing crew, and I was getting money the way I'd always been getting money—and then I guess whatever calls Def Jam had made trying to pursue the record before we'd talked ruffled some feathers with his people, and I started to get the sense that there was maybe a little friction there.

Still, the record was working, and at a certain point we popped up over at this spot called Central Station that used to be over on the south side to perform the song—as it turned out, for the first and last time, for a long, long time.

I'm honestly surprised it didn't pop off that night. Not because me and him had a personal problem, but just because of the way our people were moving. They had their straps and we had ours, and that whole night backstage you could just feel the static in the air.

Even then, I still kept doing everything I could to promote the song. I don't know if that makes me generous or solid or just whatever. Whatever it was, I just kept showing up.

He wanted to do the "So Icy (Remix)"? Cool, we did that. He wanted to shoot a video for the song? Cool, we did that.

Then my vocal cords popped.

■ ■ ■

It was Super Bowl Sunday 2005, and I was in the middle of a performance at one of Jacksonville's biggest clubs when it happened.

Now, just imagine, I'm onstage in front of a room full of people— *Trap or Die* is fresh out, and I'm the hottest thing in the streets. I'd brought two tour buses full of my people down to Florida with me, and all weekend I'd be running all over Jacksonville getting to the bag. Performances, walk-throughs, parties, afterparties, appearances, interviews. You name it, I was with it, and everywhere I went, somebody was handing me a paper bag full of cash.

What I'm saying is, I'd been going *hard*. Long nights, short days, lots of smoking and drinking, and no sleep. Sunday was the main event and the lineup that night was stacked. The promoter had billed it as The Grand Finale: Official Crunk Fest, and when I took the stage, I was ready to show out.

"Here I stand! A grown-ass man! All by myself, a grown-ass . . . !" *POP!*

I had no idea what that sound was, but I immediately knew something was wrong. It felt like someone had cut my throat with a torch. I grabbed a bottle of water off the DJ's stand and chugged, and that shit hurt like a motherfucker, too.

I went through the motions for the rest of the set, but really just let the backing track do the work. All I could think was, *Goddamn, I can't wait to get off this stage.*

By the time I got back on the bus, I couldn't talk, and that went on for weeks. I had no idea what was going on, but I knew it wasn't good. I'd been banking on my music as my way out of the streets, but how the hell was I going to ever make it as a rapper if I couldn't talk? And it's not like I had a regular doctor I could go see either. I was straight off the block and brand new to the industry. I didn't have health insurance, and I didn't have a backup plan. All I had was my story and my voice, and my voice was shot.

Those next couple of weeks were dark. To be honest, I really felt like it was my karma kicking in. I was being punished for everything I'd ever done wrong, and the punishment was that much harsher because I'd gotten so close to achieving my dreams.

Eventually Coach convinced me to go seek some help. "Don't worry about insurance," he assured me. "We'll figure it out."

I was so nervous about the whole situation that when the doctor came in to tell me the results of all the tests they'd been running, I had him step out in the hall and talk to Coach. When Coach came back into the room, I could tell by the look in his eyes that I didn't want to hear whatever he was about to say.

"Yo, Jeezy, man, so look," he said as he sat down next to my hospital bed. "They're saying you tore your vocal cords and now you have polyps on your throat. They can fix it, but they'll have to operate, and they can't say one way or another how the surgery might affect your voice."

I swear he had tears in his eyes. I probably did, too, shit. My voice was the one thing I had going for me. That was my golden ticket. In some ways, it was my gift and my curse because on the one hand that's what set me apart—every great rapper has a great voice—but on the other, it had always been a little tricky and sensitive. Even before that situation in Jacksonville, if I'd had a bunch of late nights or been doing a whole lot of shows, I'd always have to take it easy the next day and sip tea with lots of lemon in it and wait until I could really talk. Having issues with my voice was nothing new, but surgery was a whole other thing.

Still, what choice did I have? I went ahead with it, and when it came time to pay the bill, I ended up handling it just like I would have in the streets—I walked in and paid the hospital with a grocery bag full of cash.

I spent the spring of 2005 laid up, working with Mama June, one of the best vocal coaches in the game, trying to get back all the way right. I was doing my scales in the shower—straight up *fa-la-la-la-la!*—and passing notes to Nico, my engineer, so he could put the finishing touches on my Def Jam debut.

At the same time, I was canceling performances left and right, lying low, and ducking calls because I didn't want anyone in the industry to know what was going on with me. One of my biggest fears was that someone would find out I was having problems with my voice and I'd be in some type of conversation about pushing my album back or putting my deal on hold. That wasn't an option for me. The streets were a mess for real, and I didn't have time to waste.

As it turned out, some of those calls I missed were from Radric and some of his people trying to get me to do a performance for BET or something, and I guess they felt a certain kind of way when I declined because the next thing I knew, the whole city was buzzing over some song he'd put out and everybody's talking about "Gucci versus Jeezy."

I had one of my little homies bring me a copy of the record, and sure enough, there Radric was, talking all types of flagrant shit. I guess he had an album to promote or something, and he just wanted some attention. Well, shit, he got mine.

This is where I can honestly say I made a big mistake.

I let my emotions get the best of me. That's always bad—in business and in life. It took me a long time to learn that lesson because I've always run a little hot and it's never taken much to set me off, especially when it comes to giving me my respect.

Over the years, I've learned to take a beat before I act. That's not always possible, but when it is, that's what I like to do. I'll even meditate on a situation if I can. I've found taking even just a few minutes to really center yourself can help you cut through your emotions so you can clearly see your next move. But back then I wasn't quite that, let's say, *evolved*, and when I heard "Round 1," I immediately saw red. After everything I'd done for that man he was coming at me? And like that?

My throat still wasn't all the way right, but I didn't care. I hit up Nico and told him to get the studio ready. I was coming through.

■ ■ ■

"Stay Strapped" was the first song I recorded after my surgery and, like I said, looking back I can clearly see it for what it was: a mistake.

For five minutes straight over the beat to Tip's song, "ASAP," I went straight at Radric's neck. And to top it off, at the end of the record, I put a $10,000 bounty on his chain.

If I could do it all over again, I never would have put that song out. Matter of fact, I never would have recorded it in the first place because that's where I went wrong. Just by stepping in the booth that day, I gave Radric what he wanted most: attention. I was so focused on standing up and demanding my respect, I'd played right into his hands.

Once "Stay Strapped" was out, there was no going back and it wasn't long before our little local so-called "rap beef" became national news.

I can't really speak on what happened next because I wasn't there, but from what I understand the way the story is told ain't what it seems. Let's just leave it at that.

PART THREE

CHAPTER FIFTEEN

Nine Lives

Yo, was that . . . ?

I picked up the phone and called O-Dog.

"Young! Where you been hiding, bro? I ain't seen you around in a minute!"

That was true. I'd been holed up in the studio for months working on my album, and even though I'd seen a couple of people here and there, for the most part I'd been lying low. I hadn't seen O, but I had a feeling I'd just seen him ride by my crib. As far as I knew, he was the only one riding around the city in a silver BMW 745 sitting on black Giovanna rims. I should know. I'd bought mine the same day he bought his—black on black, with the black Giovannas to match.

"Yo, did I just see you ride by my crib?"

He was like, "Shit, you tell me, bro. You know I don't know where the fuck you live!"

I laughed. That was true, too. I'd known O-Dog for years, kicked it with him countless times, and made and blown so much money with him . . . shit. The money we threw in Magic City alone could have financed a local bank for real. But I'd never told him where I lived. Not once. And it wasn't just O either. *No one* knew where I lived. That was one of my cardinal rules.

Matter of fact, not even the other people who lived in the building knew I lived there. For one, I would go out of my way to make sure I ran into as few people as possible whenever I was there. The way the building was set up was great for that, with a garage in the basement and an elevator that went right to my floor. Two, the condo wasn't even in my name. Officially, like, as far as the paperwork and all that? The condo was owned by one of the guys who played for the Atlanta Braves. And as far as any of my neighbors were concerned, my name was Mike.

Well, except for this one little old lady I used to run into every now and then, coming in and out of the building's gym. She must have been in her late seventies or early eighties at the time, but she was still getting it in. She had her own personal trainer and everything. And every time she'd see me at the gym, she'd always say the same thing: "Hi, Mr. Handsome, you're here again?"

That's what she knew me as: "Mr. Handsome." To everybody else in the building, though, I was Mike.

O-Dog's voice chirped in my ear. "So what's up, though? You want to tell me where you're at or you just going to keep playing it all secret agent–like and shit?"

I thought about it for a second. I knew a storm was coming. You could feel it in the air. And I knew I only had a limited amount of time to get my shit tight before the flood came and washed everything— and everyone—away. My music was my lifeboat. It had to be. I didn't have anything else.

That's part of the reason why I hadn't seen O in so long. The streets were hot so I'd been lying low, focusing on my music. When everybody else was at the club, I was at the studio. When all types of shit were popping off in the city, I was in the studio. When I had seen O and all of them, they'd been coming by the studio after they'd all been out at the club to give me a hard time for . . . always being in the studio.

But when I called him that day, I was at home. And then I broke one of my cardinal rules. I gave him my address.

"Bet," he said. "Me and my brother are about to pull up."

■ ■ ■

I just know O-Dog and his brother looked out of place when they walked in. That building wasn't used to seeing guys in baggy-ass jeans, long white tees, and diamond chains, and braids. Shit, outside of that little old lady who knew me as "Mr. Handsome," the people who lived and worked in that building weren't even used to seeing me, and I'd lived there for years.

Still, it was great to see O. I'd recently had my condo remodeled, too, so it was my turn to do a little flex. He had his new big-ass house with his girl, and I had my multimillion-dollar bachelor pad with the fly-ass art on the walls. Like I said, we had that friendly competition thing going on, and I felt like I was raising the bar.

To be honest, they were hardly there. We chopped it up a little bit about this and that for maybe an hour or so, if that, and then they were gone. As soon as they left, though, I had this uneasy feeling, like, *Damn, I think I just made a huge mistake.*

■ ■ ■

There was one other person in the building I was cool with besides that little old lady, and it was one of the valets. He was a young cat with music dreams of his own, so he was plugged into the scene and knew me for who I really was. I used to see him out in the clubs sometimes and we'd kick it a little bit here and there. He's a good dude, and he's gone on to have a whole bunch of success managing one of the biggest R&B singers in the game.

About a week after O-Dog and his brother came through, I ran into him one night at the club. I called him over to my section and after we dapped up and all that, he leaned into my ear and said, "Yo, I just thought you should know that after your friends left the other day, all these federal agents showed up and started sweeping all your cars in the garage."

I froze. "Hold up, say that again?"

He repeated himself, and I swear it's a miracle I didn't have a heart attack right there in the club. "What you mean *federal agents*?"

"I don't know, bro," he said. "Like, I don't know if it was FBI or Homeland Security or what, but they sure looked like federal agents to me."

The next day, I got up like always. I showered, changed, grabbed my pistols and my keys, and walked out the door. I took the elevator straight down to the garage, but instead of getting into one of my cars, I walked out the garage and I just kept walking until I got to the Kroger down the road.

I hollered at one of the homies from a pay phone and told him to call the building. "Tell them we need to get some more renovations done and we're gonna have a moving company come through. Get all the art, my jewelry, and as much of the clothes and furniture as you can in one trip. Leave the rest."

After I hung up, I went and bought a bunch of those family-sized boxes of Cinnamon Toast Crunch, a case of ramen noodles, a bunch of hot sauce, and a shitload of toilet paper, paper towels, and milk. I had one of the homies come scoop me up and we went and bought about six air mattresses, a card table, some folding chairs, and a cheap-ass TV. Then me and some of my guys moved into a little three-bedroom house I had access to in Guilford Forest off of Cascade.

I had no idea what was going on, but I knew I had to tighten up. That meant no more splashing out and buying all the homies Hawaiian steaks at Houston's every night. No more buying cars straight off the lot with O-Dog and them. No more throwing all types of money in the club. No more watches, no more chains, none of that.

My album was due, but it wasn't done. The Bad Boy situation for Boyz N Da Hood was still a little up in the air. I'd put something like three million of my own money into my music, but none of it had come back to me yet, and I really was out on a ledge. On top of all of that, apparently now the feds were on my tail. I needed a plan.

■ ■ ■

That night, I tossed and turned on one of those air mattresses, wrestling with my next move. I kept thinking back on that conversation I'd had with Tip.

"The street shit and the rap shit," he'd said in that bathroom at Patchwerk. "You really can't be doing both."

I'd brushed him off at the time, but maybe he was right. The more my music was coming together, the more the street shit was falling apart. I'm not talking about the heat coming down either; I'm talking about just the way I'd been handling my business. I'd been putting so much attention on my music that I'd been letting some of the street shit slide, and I never would have done that in the past. Between the street shit and the music shit, I was working two full-time jobs and the truth was, I was shortchanging both. I wasn't as focused as I needed to be on either side. That's why the album wasn't done and that's probably why the feds were getting closer to coming through my door.

By the time the sun was creeping through the blinds, I knew what I had to do. I had to walk away from the streets. Not tomorrow or the next day or next week or next month. I had to walk away now, immediately. Like, that's it, I'm done. It was one of the hardest decisions I've ever had to make.

You've got to think, it wasn't just about me walking away from the game and everything that came with it. In a lot of ways, I was also walking away from *me*. I'd been a hustler ever since I was a kid. I didn't know any other way. I was the guy with the Ferraris and the watches and the chains. I was the guy throwing all that money in the club, dipping in and out of state making plays, looking at all the rappers walking around like, *Man, that dude ain't got shit on me*. I was Lil' J, Bling, the big homie on the low.

Last time I checked, I was the man on these streets . . .

And you're telling me—*I* was telling me—that all of that was done? That was a hard transition to make, and even harder for me to accept. I'd be in the studio and see a number pop up on my phone and just know it was somebody calling me about a play, and it would take everything I had in me not to answer that call. I quit the game cold turkey, and I was mad at myself about that decision for a long, long time.

Then the indictments started coming down and everybody around me started going to jail.

■ ■ ■

Gold Mouth got locked up first—not like *first*-first because the way I came up, people around me had been getting locked up my whole life. But in terms of people in my true inner circle, Gold Mouth was the first. And I swear Cuzzo was involved in that, too.

This was back when we were still doing good business, or at least I thought we were. He was working with one of my other cousins, and they had a line on some things, so Gold Mouth and I would dip up to Atlanta to get right and then fly back down to Macon to get it off. Well, one time when we went up there, I had a few things I was handling in the city on the side—some music, some street—so Gold Mouth was like, "I got this, cuz. You stay up here and do what you need to do."

When I got back to Macon, Gold Mouth wasn't answering his phone. It wasn't like him to be out of pocket like that, and it felt so off, I ended up sitting in my car outside my crib for hours debating what to do. Eventually, I decided to check myself into a hotel room to wait it out. When my phone rang the next day, one of my other cousins was on the line talking about, "Hey, man, you know Gold Mouth in jail?"

I had my lawyer go down and pay his bail, and when I picked Gold Mouth up, he really wasn't even tripping all that much, which surprised me because I was worried as hell. Turns out for good reason, too. On the way back home, Gold Mouth told me that when they stopped him, they knew exactly where to look. Not only that, but they knew the rendezvous spot was right down the street from my crib. Matter of fact, they took him over there in the back of an unmarked car so they could try to pop me.

"And you know what's crazy, cuz?" he said. "You pulled up right next to us at a red light, and I tried my best not to look at you, I swear. But then you pulled off and we just kept going."

That moment said a lot—a lot about Gold Mouth's character and a lot about loyalty overall. All he had to do was point me out, and you just know he would have had a much easier time. But he stayed loyal and kept his mouth shut—just like Mrs. Mattie Pickett had taught me way back in the day—and even when they took him over to my spot, he just kept playing dumb.

Gold Mouth ended up doing ten years behind that, and by the time he got out, I had two platinum albums out with another one on the way. But instead of holding my success against me or harboring any type of resentment, he told me he spent a lot of his time inside talking me up and defending my name and letting any of the haters know that I really was who I said I was. I can't tell you how much respect I have for him for all of that and how much I appreciate the sacrifice he made and how grateful I am for his genuine love because he easily could have played it a whole other way.

As for Cuzzo and my other cousin and them? I can't say for sure that they had something to do with it, but there were the four of us who knew what was going on and the heat came down on Gold Mouth and me, so to me, that's simple math. I will say that's another one of those moments that stuck with me and made it so I didn't feel too bad about the move I made against him later on.

■ ■ ■

Mel Man's situation was a bit more complicated, and in some ways made me feel even worse because he really got caught up in something that was intended for me.

This was another one of those situations that happened in Macon. I was dealing with this cat Bobby and he was from another 'hood, but he was a Crip, too. Bobby was the breakdown man. Everything he bought, he was breaking it down, breaking down.

Anyway, one day I was over at one of the shotgun homes we used to stay at on Madden Avenue when Bobby called, and I had him come meet me over there. When I stepped out to see him, I happened to look down the road, and that's when I saw this unmarked car just sitting there, backed into one of the drives. As soon as I saw it, I took off running straight through the woods behind the house, and I just kept going.

Well, a couple of weeks later, we were back to business as usual, but when he hit me up, I was out of town. I hadn't put two and two together, so I had Mel Man go holler at him and Mel Man was so reliable, I didn't think much of it until all these hours started going by and he wasn't answering his phone. Finally, one of the homies hit me up like, "Yo, I just seen your guy pulled over by the side of the road. Looked like they had him in handcuffs."

"Man, what?" I wasn't prepared for that.

Then, it just went from bad to worse. Mel Man was living with this white chick in the suburbs at the time, and their whole situation seemed toxic. She was rowdy as hell, and I'd tell him all the time, "Yo, man, you can't have her all in your business."

She used to always think he was cheating on her, too, so when he didn't come home, she started blowing up his phone and when one of the female officers answered, that just set her off. She got on that ra-ra, *Here's my address if you want to come see me, we can go right now*–type shit like she wanted to fight, and when the cops pulled up and started going through the house, they found everything Mel Man was holding for me in the attic. I'm talking money, guns, and all types of shit. He ended up doing about ten years off that, and even though we're cool now, it's not like how it was when Gold Mouth came home. With Mel Man, there was a little more friction, and all I can say is that I get it. I really do.

Both of those situations were fucked up. On the one hand, that's just a day in the life, but on the other I could never shake it off the same way I could some other things. *Damn, I'm glad it wasn't me* didn't work when it came to them.

Mel Man and Gold Mouth getting locked up is probably one of my biggest regrets, if not *the* biggest regret, about everything I've ever done. Not because I could have changed anything about either of those specific situations, but when I think back on it, I do blame myself for putting them on that road. When we first started out, we were just kids, and they had their own paths and dreams. I was the criminal, and because we were friends, they were just trying to help me.

■ ■ ■

In June 2005, they got O-Dog in the Old Fourth Ward and charged him with cocaine trafficking. Turns out they'd had his phone, his brother's phone, and his brother's girlfriend's phones tapped for months. That was the first big moment where it was like, hold up, what the fuck is going on?

Then they got Bleu DaVinci's little brother, Baby Bleu, and charged him with aggravated assault after saying he had something to do with Bobby Brown's nephew getting stabbed in the neck at a party at Justin's in May. The crazy thing about that, though, was that the day after Baby Bleu was indicted, some paperwork popped up talking about some outstanding FBI warrant for his arrest, which just showed the feds were watching for real, for real.

A week after *that*, O-Dog was sentenced to fifteen years and his plea agreement mentioned something about a RICO case, which is what the feds typically use to take down operations like the mob. No one knew it at the time, but apparently O-Dog had been talking, too, but just hearing that RICO thing, it was like, *Dog, this shit is serious.*

Then I got word that the US Marshals raided a house in the north Dallas suburbs and grabbed Meech along with some other guys. They'd found some weed, some guns, and some pills in the house, but to be honest, when I first heard the news, I brushed it off. It was like when the world first heard that 'Pac had been shot in Vegas. He'd already been through so much you sort of just assumed he would survive. By that point, it was like, *'Pac's invincible, right?*

Well, it was the same thing with Meech. He'd already had all these run-ins with the law, but no matter what they threw at him, they could never get anything to stick. He was just one of those Teflon Don types, like a cat with nine lives. I knew it was only a matter of time before they either dismissed the charges or one of the other guys who'd been in the house stepped up to take the fall. But as the weeks wore on and Meech didn't come home, I started to get that feeling like, *Damn, this might be something else.*

Then they got Meech's brother, Terry, in St. Louis, and the DEA issued a press release the very next day.

DEA Deals Motor City Mafia a Knock-Out Blow

Detroit Drug Legends Facing Twenty Years to Life

OCT. 28, 2005—(Washington, DC)—The Drug Enforcement Administration (DEA) dealt a knock-out blow to the self-named Black Mafia Family (BMF) arresting 30 individuals and seizing $3 million in currency and assets, 2 1/2 kilograms of cocaine and numerous weapons. The BMF was a large-scale cocaine trafficking and money laundering organization operating a criminal enterprise in Detroit, MI; Atlanta and Columbus, GA; Los Angeles, CA; Miami, Ft. Lauderdale, and Orlando, FL; St. Louis, MO; Greenville, SC; and Louisville, KY. Prior to today's arrests, DEA and state and local authorities had arrested 17 BMF members and associates and seized 632 kilograms of cocaine, $5.3 million in U.S. currency and $5.7 million in assets.

After that, all hell broke loose, and it happened so quick that I was a little caught off guard. The way I'd been brought up, you lived by a code, but as soon as Meech and all of them got locked up, it seemed like whatever code I'd thought we were living by went right out the window. Next thing I knew, I was in an all-out war and having full-fledged shootouts on sight with cats who'd told me just the other day that we were brothers and that they loved me. It was crazy, and the only way I could understand it was to think that just because cats had been seeing me around, they thought they knew my heart, but they didn't know my past.

After the first couple of little incidents, I took three tour buses down to Macon and I brought the whole 'hood back up to Atlanta. Then I went and bought a ten-bedroom mansion in the suburbs and put everybody up, and for the next few years, I had damn near a hundred people and a hundred guns with me everywhere I went.

Meanwhile, because so many people I knew got swept up all at once, I was talking to my friends' families and kids, trying to console them, and doing everything I could to make sure they were straight. At the same time, I was suffering because all my friends were gone so of course I was missing them, too. It's one thing to have that *Damn I'm glad it wasn't me* mantra to fall back on when it's one or two people you know going down, but when it's everybody all at once it's just like, *Damn, that's a lot.*

And then every time I sat down for an interview, it seemed like the only thing anybody wanted to know about me was: *What's your relationship with BMF?*

■ ■ ■

First things first: I was never a BMF artist and I never did a deal with BMF Entertainment. I know a lot of people assumed that's what was going on, including a lot of people in the crew, but that was never the case. We were always our own separate entities.

Now, does BMF hold the same place in the culture if I hadn't been right there standing next to them making all those songs? I don't know. And you could ask the same question about me. A lot of people do, and I can't fault them for it either, but the truth is, we'll never know because it's impossible to take our stories apart. But we never did a deal.

It did come up, though—once. I was over at Meech's stepdad's house on the east side, which is where Meech and his mom used to host their Thanksgiving dinners every year. That was always a great day—plenty of food, brotherhood, and love. Hanging with Meech and them really was like being a part of a family, so much so that his mom became almost like a second mother to me, and she still calls me "son" to this day.

Meech had a pool table in the basement, but that's also where he kept all his guard dogs. And they were trained attack dogs, too, like the ones the Secret Service has. They were ferocious. He kept them in kennels, and every time we'd go down there to shoot pool, I always felt like Meech had an edge because whenever you'd go to take a shot, those dogs would just start losing their minds.

One day when I was still going back and forth with Def Jam on the details of the deal, I was over at the house and this New York cat who used to run with them asked me to come downstairs. He had a reputation for being a wild dude and I'd heard enough to know that he'd earned it, too.

When we got downstairs, he threw a Louis Vuitton duffel on the pool table and said he wanted me to sign with BMF. As soon as that bag hit the table, those dogs started barking up a storm.

I was like, "Man, I appreciate it, but I'm good."

He unzipped the bag. There must have been something like two million in cash in there at least.

"I'm not asking, I'm telling you," he said. "We want you to sign with us."

I started looking for the exits, any loose pool cues lying around, anything that might give me an advantage. Of course, I had that thing on me, but I didn't want to take it there unless that's where it had to go. I stood firm.

"I'm saying, I appreciate what you're talking about and all that, but I've got this Def Jam situation going on and I'm planning on doing that."

I knew he was about that trigger play and I could tell he was getting hot. "Like I said, I'm not asking," he said, through his teeth. "You're signing with *us*."

But I wasn't backing down, and once I'd made that crystal clear, he let it go. At the end of the day, it was about maintaining my integrity and all of the hard work I'd already put in on my own. I wasn't trying to sign with anybody. No matter what it cost me, I was determined to come into the music game on my own two feet.

CHAPTER SIXTEEN

Soul Survivor

When Akon's brother, Bu, pulled up outside of Patchwerk that night, I ran out to meet him in my socks.

"Yo, 'Kon told me to give this to you," he said, handing me a CD through the window of his BMW 645. "I think there's something like six beats on there. He thought you might be fucking with a few."

When I went back inside, I had Nico throw it on. Akon had sent over some fire that's for damn sure, but it was the second-to-last beat that really spoke to me. I told Nico, "Yo, let's do this one real quick before I hit the club."

I was still messing with the first verse when Shake walked in about a half hour later, and as soon as he heard what we were working on, he was like, "Yo, this shit is hard!"

I kept at it until I felt like we had that verse in a good place, and then we hit up Vision and balled the fuck out. It must have been something like four or five hours later when we fell back into Patchwerk. Everybody was charged up and I was ready to work.

I told Nico to find something for me real quick and as he was going through beats looking for something that felt right, Shake was like, "Yo, why don't you just finish that song you were working on?"

"That's why they pay you the big bucks, huh?" I said, fucking with him.

He poured himself a drink. "I ain't never told you nothing wrong."

Crazy thing was, he was right.

Nico brought Akon's beat back up, and I went into the booth and did my thing. By the time I came out, Shake was hype.

"This is it, bro!" he said, slapping the board as Nico played it back. "This is *it!*"

I wasn't sure. The song sounded a little too commercial to me and that was always a real source of tension between the label and me. Def Jam was always pushing me to make songs that could work on the radio, but I wasn't interested in radio play if I felt like I had to sell out the culture or my sound to get it.

I've always wanted my music to stand for something and to speak for the streets. My favorite artist of all time is 'Pac, so coming up, he was the blueprint. One of the things that made 'Pac great was that he never compromised himself, his values, or his art just to sell some records. He was on a different mission, and he kept it all the way real, no matter the consequences. If you ask me, that's a big part of why millions of people all over the world still love and respect him to this day. So every time I'd end up in those conversations with Def Jam about putting the album out, and it would always come back to, *Well, we need a single*, it would make me so mad because I felt like they didn't understand what I was really all about.

On a certain level, making music just to get some radio play just seems desperate to me, almost like you're begging people to like you. And that definitely wasn't me. At the same time, to me it was just like, if I did step out of character on a song and it really worked, then what? I'd have all these fans loving me for being someone different from who I really was? Nah, that wasn't going to work.

My name was buzzing and I had all these people riding with me because I was who I said I was. I am the truth. So even though Shake loved the song, coming out of that session that night, I wasn't sure. Matter of fact, I don't know if I ever would have gotten on the same page with Def Jam about it if the album hadn't leaked when it did. Of course, as soon as that happened, going back and forth with the label about a single was the last thing on my mind.

■ ■ ■

I was just waking up when one of the homies hit me with the news. "Yo, Young, your whole album's out."

"You're fucking with me, right?" I wiped the sleep from my eyes and checked the time. It was late afternoon, and for the first time in months, I felt like I'd actually slept.

He was like, "I wish I was." By the time he'd finished filling me in, I was already out the door and gunning it down I-75, headed straight to Patchwerk in a blue Porsche truck Meech had given me, tears in my eyes.

They say you spend your whole life writing your first album, right? Well, even though I already had a few albums out, my Def Jam debut was going to be my first real album in my eyes. I'd put my whole life into it. All the ups and downs, all the trials and tribulations, the sacrifice, the success, the pain. I was planning on calling it *Let's Get It: Thug Motivation 101*. And it was the truth—*my* truth—and I'd given that album my all.

I knew that album was my one shot to get out of the life I was in. Any pressure I'd felt when I first started thinking about getting into music, way back in Macon, was ten thousand times more intense now. My music was my ticket to a better life—and even if I never made it to that better life, my music was my story, and that made that collection of songs invaluable to me. Matter of fact, I was so precious about it and so focused on making sure that no matter what happened to me, those songs and my story survived, that whenever I'd fly up to New York to meet with the label, I'd always put one of my guys on a separate flight with a copy of the album, just in case something happened to my plane.

That's what had leaked that day. That album was my life. And I knew just who'd done it, too.

There was this one goofy-ass engineer over at Patchwerk who'd tried to submit some beats for the album, and ever since I was basically like thanks, but no thanks, he'd been acting funny. I'd been keeping my masters at the studio, and I couldn't think of anyone else over there who would want to do something like that to me. To be honest, I couldn't think of anyone else who would even try.

When I pulled up, I saw his goofy ass standing right outside Patchwerk's door, and I hopped out the truck with that thing in my hand, ready to let it go.

One of the homies I'd called from the road hollered out, "Don't do it, Young! Don't do it!"

I looked and before I even realized that they'd pulled up right behind me, they were on that goofy-ass engineer's ass.

He shook loose and took off, darting through traffic with the homies on his tail. Meanwhile, I was trying to get a bead on the dude, and the whole situation was fucking with my line of sight.

I yelled out, "Yo, y'all better get out the way or I'ma pop you, too!"

That's when my guy Slick Pulla grabbed him and just started beating him down, right there in the middle of traffic. I put my thing up and got out there with him and we all went to work. I promise you by the time we were done, he knew he'd tried the wrong one.

■ ■ ■

I spent the next two months doing everything I could to try to stop the leak. At one point, I even had a van full of homies all strapped with AKs running up on all the major bootleggers in the city like, "You better come up off that Young Jeezy album, and we better not catch you selling any more of them, either!"

But there was nothing to be done.

By the time I was waiting in the wings at Birthday Bash 10—thinking about how I'd gone from standing in the parking lot handing out *Tha Streets Iz Watchin* to being one of the headlining acts the very next year—the leak had spread so far, so fast that when my DJ accidentally dropped the instrumental to "Bottom of the Map," it felt like every single one of the 20,000 fans knew every line. I swear, the whole crowd was rapping the song.

> It's Young Jizzle from the bottom of the map!
> Got a 50-round clip on the bottom of the strap!
> Hey!
> I do it for the trappers with the, the, the rocks!
> And the O.G. niggas with the, the, the blocks!
> Hey!

I thought I was going to be sick. The official release date for *Thug Motivation* was still three days away, but if that many people already knew the words like *that*, I just knew there was no way in hell the album would sell.

But then the craziest thing happened. The leak helped.

I never would have guessed it, but after the leak gave the fans a taste of what I was working on, they let us know what they liked and what they didn't like, and that feedback was invaluable. That's how I found out that even the East Coast hip-hop heads couldn't front on "Go Crazy," and those were some of my toughest critics, by the way.

And the leak let me know that everyone, everywhere, was feeling the Akon record. I'd called it "Soul Survivor."

When the Def Jam people got wind of the response, they told me, "Look, you can do what you want, but this is the song we're running with."

"Soul Survivor" ended up being the album's second single and in the fall of 2005, that song was everywhere. I'm talking MTV, BET, rap radio, pop, crossover, top five on the *Billboard* charts—all of it. The success of "Soul Survivor" surprised everyone, including me. Everyone that is, except for Shake. He'd immediately heard it for what it was—a hit. And not just a hit, but a smash.

■ ■ ■

"What's really good, Atlanta?!" Shake yelled. "Y'all having a good time?"

It was July 25, 2005, and *Let's Get It: Thug Motivation 101* was officially in stores, and that was something to celebrate for real. I'd spent the whole day running all over the city doing promo and interviews and getting everything ready for the album release party that night.

The *Trap or Die* release had gone so well that I wanted to run that same play for *Thug Motivation*, but leveled up. Same venue, same full-court-press strategy. Just even bigger and better than before. There was just one thing: the promoter at Vision wasn't so sure people would really come out on a Tuesday in the middle of the summer, just a couple of days after Birthday Bash.

But I knew what I had and I wasn't concerned. I told him, "Look, how 'bout you don't pay me anything for the event and just let me get the door and thirty percent of the bar?"

He was like, "I can't do thirty. Twenty."

"Bet."

I flooded the city with flyers. I'm talking I put 400,000 of them out there letting the whole world know that the night *Thug Motivation* dropped, Vision was going up. That campaign damn sure worked, too. When I rode by Vision something like three hours before the event, there were so many people already lined up, you would have thought they were giving away free Jordans at the club. It was so crazy, I had my driver double back just so I could get a better look. I still didn't know if the album would sell, *But if nothing else*, I thought, *I'm going to make a killing at the club.*

Hours later, Shake was standing on top of one of the banquets yelling into the mic.

"Def Jam is in the building! My man Jay-Z is in the building! Beyoncé is in the building! What's up, girl? I see you!"

And she was, too. They both were. Everybody was there.

"B! M! F! is in the building! *Big Meech* is in the building! The *Snoooooow-mannnn* is in the building!"

I held up the gold bottle in my hand and the cameras flashed all in my face as everybody screamed. Shake kept going, drink in one hand, mic in the other.

"Who in here got that *Thug Motivation* album?"

The crowd screamed some more.

"That's what's up!" Shake said. "So I want everybody in here to raise a bottle or a glass or whatever you're drinking, and give it up to my guy Young Jeezy who just signed The! Biggest! Record deal! In-the-motherfucking-world! One hundred million dollars for Young Jeezy and C! T! EEEEEE! Play that shit! Let's get it!"

The DJ dropped "Bottom of the Map" and the club went on tilt. Meanwhile, I saw all the homies looking at me like I was food— lunch *and* dinner. Even my sister was looking at me crazy.

I grabbed Shake by the collar and pulled him down toward me. "Yo, why the fuck would you say some shit like that when you know it isn't true?"

Shake just looked at me and laughed. "We gotta sell this shit, baby!" he said as he reached for another bottle of champagne. That was the thing about Shake: he knew how to make everything larger than life.

CHAPTER SEVENTEEN

Marketing 101

"Yo, how much for that watch?"

I pointed at the gold Presidential Rolex with the green face and the iced-out baguettes on the bezel in the display case.

Fevzi Aydin looked at me from behind the counter and laughed. This was back when he still had his shop at the Apparel Mart in downtown Atlanta and years before Fevzi Made It became one of the city's marquee jewelers.

"I'm not sure if that's the one for you, little man," he said, and went back to doing whatever he was doing before I walked in.

I was fourteen, maybe fifteen years old at the time, straight out the 'Ville, and barely tall enough to see over the case. But I was sure. "How much?"

"Fifteen thousand," he said with that tone like, *We done here?*

I pulled fifteen racks out of my pocket and put them on the counter. "I'll take it."

After that, I started going to see Fevzi whenever I was feeling flush.

Over the years, he hooked me up with everything from Rollies to diamond earrings to chains, and I had him flood a few watches for me and things like that. But I'd never gone to see him about building something for me from scratch until after "Dem Boyz" and "Icy" started moving. The way I was looking at it, with so many other street-type rappers coming out at the time and everybody wearing nothing but white and black tees, I needed a statement piece to help me stand out.

I pulled up on him one day in late 2004 and did a quick sketch. "This is what I want," I told him, turning the paper around so he could see.

He looked at my simple drawing of a snowman for a minute and then was just like, "No problem. Give me three weeks."

When I went back to get it, and he took it out and laid it on the counter, that piece was so cold, just seeing it gave me chills. He'd flooded the snowman with ice and set it on a solitary diamond chain. Even more than that, though, he'd taken my vision and made it real. When I tell you my confidence was on 100 trillion when I walked out of his shop with that chain on, man, what? You couldn't tell me nothing! The way I was feeling, the Snowman was in town, and you better respect it or check it.

Funny thing about it, though, I can't tell you how many times somebody walked up to me in the club like, "Yo, that moneybag chain is *crazy*!"

And every time, it was just like, *moneybag*? But as more and more people got exposed to my music and started to understand who I was, any confusion melted away. Then, when all the people I'd been running with stopped calling me Jeezy or Lil' J and started calling me Snow, I knew the snowman piece had taken on a life of its own.

One day, Tip hit me up like, "Yo, Young, that snowman shit is genius!"

I laughed. "What you mean *genius*?"

He was like, "It's genius, bro. It's great marketing."

Until he said it, I really hadn't been thinking about it on those terms. To be honest, at the time, I really didn't even know to think about it in those terms. I didn't know anything about marketing campaigns—good or bad. I was just trying to do something to set myself apart that felt right to me.

Then, one day not too long after that, I was up in the Def Jam offices having another one of those meetings about selling my music that I wasn't really trying to have because they always seemed to involve some version of me selling out, when the conversation shifted to trying to find some type of gimmick to help sell *Thug Motivation 101*.

This was back when Mike Jones was popping, and he had his whole thing where he'd shout out his real phone number in his songs. It was like an early viral marketing campaign, and the people up at Def Jam were trying to come up with something like that for me.

We were sitting around a conference table with those floor-to-ceiling Midtown Manhattan views I'd expected the first time I met with L.A. Reid, and everybody was talking, batting around ideas, and as I looked out at all those skyscrapers, I thought about what Tip had said—*that's great marketing*. I took my snowman chain off and held it up so everybody at the table could see.

"Why don't we just use this?"

■ ■ ■

There were a hundred shirts in the first run of the Snowman tees. The label printed them up based on a design that Def Jam's marketing director Ashaunna Ayars quickly sketched out in that conference room and Eif Rivera, who was working in the Def Jam art department at the time, refined.

Those first hundred tees went so quick, I went in my pocket and printed up five hundred more. I couldn't give everybody who wanted to get down with my movement an iced-out Snowman chain, but I could give them a Snowman tee, so that's what I did. I started handing out Snowman tees everywhere I went, and whenever I ran out, I printed up some more.

We must have put fifty thousand Snowman tees on the streets in the spring of 2005 alone. By the time *Thug Motivation* came out, the Snowman tee was in high demand. I remember Juelz Santana wore it in one of his videos, and I even heard that Kanye West asked Def Jam to make him one custom—black on black on black. I guess you could call it the Yeezy x Jeezy Snowman tee. Just imagine how much that would go for today.

Of course, with the Snowman tee jumping like that, the bootleggers were out in force, too, to the point where one day I was riding down Bankhead with my man and we passed a homeless guy rocking one. To be honest, that didn't sit right with me at first, and I told my man, "Yo, we should go back around and take that shirt."

My man looked at me, and then he was just like, "Nah, bro, that's a good look. We want everybody to represent."

For me, that's when it really hit home. I'd been looking at the Snowman as a reflection of me, but what my man understood was that the Snowman had become bigger than Young Jeezy, the artist. The Snowman had become an idea, all about making something out of nothing, standing tall and hustling your way to the top, no matter the odds. The Snowman was the people's champ. The ultimate hustler. And when people put that Snowman tee on, they were telling the world that they aspired to be the ultimate hustler, too.

The dopest thing about it was that idea was rooted in my message. That's all I've ever been about and that's all I ever wanted anybody to get from being around me: Inspiration. Motivation. Hustle. The truth.

I leaned back in the passenger's seat, confident that my message and my movement were growing, and no matter who was rocking it, everybody who needed to know knew that the idea of the Snowman was rooted in me.

■ ■ ■

When *Thug Motivation* came out, the Snowman was right there, printed on the CD. I'm talking on the disc itself so every time you threw it on, and this was back when you still had to put CDs on, you saw the Snowman. I'd been worried that all the bootlegging would eat into my sales, but the album still sold 172,000 copies in its first week of release and debuted at number two on the *Billboard* charts.

Those next few weeks after the album dropped were a blur. I did *Jimmy Kimmel Live!* in LA. I shot the "Soul Survivor" video in New York. Then I was down in Miami for the MTV Video Music Awards, and the whole time *Thug Motivation* kept jumping off the shelves. I can't say how many more copies we would have sold if the album hadn't leaked, but we sold two-million-plus regardless, and the Snowman tee was everywhere.

I remember stopping by some streetwear shop up in Harlem during a promo run and they had a whole wall full of nothing but variations of the Snowman tee. There was the classic one we'd done, but also a Puerto Rican Snowman, the Snowman in a Yankees jersey, a Rasta Snowman, the Snowman holding an AK, and all these other types. It was wild.

Not too long after that, Jay-Z invited me to MAGIC.

"It's in Vegas," he said. "You should come."

I was like, "Cool. I'm with it. What's Magic?"

■ ■ ■

The first time I met Jay-Z was in early 2005. I was standing outside the Def Jam building with something like fifty to a hundred guys because that's how I was rolling everywhere I went. The streets were *hot* and I was on, and I wasn't about to let anybody catch me slipping—no way, nowhere, no how. You know how rappers are a little notorious for having an entourage? Yeah, well, I had a mob.

Jay pulled up in a black-on-black Maybach, and when he stepped out and saw me, he hollered, like, "Yo, Jeezy! Let's go upstairs."

At that point, Jay was just a couple of weeks into his new role as Def Jam's new president and CEO, and we went up to his office and chopped it up. We didn't even really talk about music that day. It was more so a meeting where we were feeling each other out. I think he wanted to see if I was really who I said I was, and to be honest, I was sort of doing the same thing with him. It's one thing to see somebody on TV and in magazines and to listen to their music; it's another to sit down and talk one-on-one.

By the time I left his office, we'd built a natural connection and I knew that we would be able to have conversations about things that went way beyond the music business. And that's exactly how it played out, too. From that point on, whenever we linked up, we hardly ever talked about songs or album rollouts or any of that. For the most part our conversations were always about where we are, where we're headed, and where we're trying to go next as men.

Hov did help a whole lot on the music side, too, though, don't get me wrong. For one, I don't think the whole Boyz N Da Hood situation would have worked out in quite the same way if Jay hadn't stepped into his new role when he did.

Puff had been on me about it all fall trying to get me to close the deal. The thing was, he wanted me to commit to four albums with the group, and that didn't really interest me so I negotiated. I told him, "Look, if you can get me that same number to do one album, I can fuck with that."

Puff made the numbers work, but after *Trap or Die* blew up and I disappeared for a minute to have my surgery, all of a sudden there started to be a whole lot of conflict around the release dates. Puff wanted the Boyz N Da Hood album to come out in late June, but we'd been talking about putting my album out in early July and everybody up at Def Jam was concerned that back-to-back releases might be too much Young Jeezy for the market to bear. I can't say I was too thrilled about it either. If all the fans rushed out to buy the Boyz N Da Hood album and skipped mine because they'd already spent all their money on that, that wasn't going to work.

So, I did what I always do in those types of situations: I came up with a plan.

I knew Jay and Puff already had a good rapport, so I got Jay, Puff, and L.A. Reid on the phone and told them, "I think I see a way this can be good for all of us. Why don't we have Puff put out the Boyz N Da Hood album in June like he wants, and then we push my album back a couple of weeks and use the group album to promote my solo release?"

Jay was like, "Oh, you're really smart, huh?"

L.A. loved the idea. "That's fucking genius! Who's telling you this?"

"Nobody," I told him. "It just feels like the right thing to do."

Of course, Puff was with it because nothing had to change on his end, so that's what we did. The Boyz N Da Hood album came out on June 21, 2005, and sold 110,000 copies in its first week of release. It was Bad Boy's first number-one album on the rap charts in two years and the fifth biggest album in the country overall. By the end of the summer, I was a debut artist with two major label deals and two top-five albums to my name. I can't think of another artist out there who can make that claim, and for the most part I'd negotiated that whole situation, built my own buzz, connected the dots, paid my own way, and set everything up all on my own.

"Oh, you're really smart, huh?" Hov had said at the time.

I may not be perfect—far from it—but I'm definitely not dumb.

■ ■ ■

Over the years, I've made some classic records with Hov like "Go Crazy," the "My President Is Black (Remix)," and "Seen It All." Matter of fact, "Go Crazy" is another one of those positive things that ended up coming out of the album leak. Jay wasn't on the original version, but after he saw the response, especially on the East Coast, he hopped on. I've rocked stadiums and been all over the country with him on tour, and we've had countless great conversations and more than a few epic nights.

He's been there for me on some of my most challenging days, looked out for me in ways big and small, and always been there to lend an ear or offer me some guidance if he thought he had it to give. I'll always have nothing but respect for him for that—all of it.

To be honest, in a lot of ways more than anyone else I've ever met—and certainly more than anyone else I've ever met in the music industry—being around Jay has always reminded me of what it was like being around Meech. Not in what they do because they move in different ways, but in the sense that they're both a little older than me and they've both got that deeper perspective because they've both seen more of the game. And just like Meech, Jay is always dropping gems, so if you stick around, listen close, and pay attention, you just might pick up a few things that could change your life.

That's why my ears perked up when he invited me to MAGIC. Like I said, though, there was just one thing: "What's Magic?"

■ ■ ■

MAGIC is the Men's Apparel Guild in California, and it's a week-long fashion trade show that takes over the Las Vegas Convention Center twice a year. That's where all the brands and all the buyers for all the major retailers meet up and do business. I sort of knew it was a big deal walking in, but I was not prepared for the size of that show.

The Las Vegas Convention Center has over 2.5 million square feet of exhibition space, and I swear every single one of them was being put to use. Everywhere you looked—I'm talking wall to wall, floor to ceiling, the rafters, *everywhere*—all you saw were clothes and clothing brands. From the biggest brands in the world to the guys making T-shirts out of their garage, they were all there.

And it was a zoo.

Shake flew out to Vegas with me, and as soon as we walked in, it was just like, *Goddamn!*

Jay and his partner Dame Dash were making a killing with their clothing line, Rocawear, at the time, and it felt like it took us damn near half the day just to find their booth. When we finally did, I posted up with my eyes and ears open, soaking up the game. I'd showed up at MAGIC feeling like the music business was the biggest thing in the world, but I could tell by the scope of everything that was going on that fashion was on a whole other plane. Just to put some numbers on it: in 2020, the global music industry was estimated to be worth roughly $26 billion. That same year, the global fashion industry was estimated to be worth $2.5 *trillion*. I don't know what the numbers were back then, but I could see that there were levels. And I had a whole lot to learn.

At a certain point, Jay came over to me like, "Yo, let's walk the floor and check out the show."

That was a dope experience. Just think, in two years I'd gone from trying to get anyone, anywhere, to listen to *Come Shop Wit Me* to walking the MAGIC floor with Jay-Z. I was loving every minute of it. And what was even crazier was that it seemed like we couldn't go ten steps without somebody coming up to thank *me*.

The first couple of times it happened, I just sort of brushed it off thinking they were just fans of my music, but it got to the point where I just knew there had to be something else going on. Finally, I asked this young Filipino cat, like, "Man, thank me for what?"

"For the Snowman shirts, bro!" he said. "Everybody's caking off of those this year. We're all going to eat!"

"Hold up," I said, and that's when it hit me. I stepped out of my *look-how-far-I've-made-it* thoughts and really scanned the room. Sure enough, in damn near every booth, everywhere I looked, there were all these flips of the Snowman tee hanging on racks and piled in boxes from here to the moon.

Jay looked at me. "Yo, I hope you trademarked that," he said.

As much as I hated to admit it, I hadn't. If I had, I probably could have made more off the Snowman tee in 2005 alone than I ever would have made off of music. But by the time we were at MAGIC, that ship had sailed. It was like the *Thug Motivation* bootlegs all over again. Even if I did try to run up on everyone with a van full of goons, we'd never get that cat back in the bag. That Filipino dude was right, though. Everybody was going to eat off the Snowman tee that year. Everybody, that is, except me.

If I could do it all over again, of course I'd go back and trademark the Snowman as soon as I had Fevzi make that first chain. And I'd trademark every iteration of the Snowman that came after it, too. But you don't know what you don't know, and as simple as it sounds, you really do have to live and learn. At the same time, you have to be able to accept the wins and the losses. And through it all, you've got to keep the faith.

Even though it's easy to say I would go back and do things differently if I could, who's to say that would have been the right thing to do? Maybe not having the Snowman trademark in place is exactly what my career needed at the time because it allowed the Snowman to spread. Either way, it was bad business, that's for damn sure, but it was great marketing. There's no denying that.

CHAPTER EIGHTEEN

The Inspiration

I started working on my next album pretty much as soon as *Thug Motivation* came out. In early 2006, I moved everything down to Miami and posted up at South Beach Studios, which was this spot that used to be an old Art Deco hotel just off the beach. That studio was dope. It wasn't as fly as some of the city's splashier joints, but I liked it because it was so low-key and in the cut. It was also super close to Mansion, which was one of South Beach's biggest clubs. South Beach Studios wasn't Patchwerk—Patchwerk is a one of one—but I was comfortable there and I was able to work.

One Friday night, Shake pulled up on me rocking these two big-ass gold-and-diamond chains, like, "What's really good?" As soon as I saw him shining like that, I knew it was going to be one of those nights.

I was hosting a party at Mansion that night, and it was a light show as soon as we walked into the room. Shake had his two chains on, and of course everything I had on was ice cold. The girls had the sparklers in the air, the gold bottles were almost as cold as my chains, and our section was set up—it was the extra-extra VIP treatment. That was the new standard.

But as we headed to our section, I saw Bleu DaVinci posted up with some of his people, and I just knew it was going to be a problem. It wasn't that we had beef, exactly. It was more so that he was just on that list of cats who I knew was feeling some type of way because of everything that had been going on. And then that was especially true with him because for BMF Entertainment, he was supposed to be the one, and even though I felt like I'd done everything I could to help him out, for whatever reasons, the music thing wasn't really working for him, and it was working for me.

So if you ask me, that's where the static was coming from. And as we were leaving the club, some words were exchanged and the next thing you know, everybody was out in the street in the middle of this big-ass brawl. I was so sick of people playing with me. There was no way I was about to back down, and then cats started letting them things go. I'm talking firecrackers right there in the middle of South Beach like it's nothing.

Pop-pop-pop-pop-pop-pop!

I jumped into one of the Lincoln Navigators we were rolling in that night. It was me, Shake, this cat we used to call Shitty Strap because of the way he used to sneak his gun into the club, and this cat I knew from LA who'd actually been kicking it with Bleu but had hopped in the truck with me, like, "Yo, he was wrong for that shit."

Then the cops lit us up—*woop, woop!*

That's when the LA cat told me he still had his gun. I was like, "Man, are you serious?"

Next thing I knew, the police had us lying on the ground right in the middle of South Beach and all these people were riding by hollering out their windows like, "Oh, shit! They locking up Jeezy!"

They found two guns in the car that night—the LA cat's and Shake's—but they decided to try to put both of them on me. I'll never forget it either. I was lying there, facedown on the concrete, when the cop walked over and took out his cuffs, like, "So, we found two firearms in the vehicle, and it's your lucky day, Snowman. They're yours."

Four people in the car, but I guess since I was the big rap star, I was the big prize and they were going to do everything they could to make an example out of me.

I ended up sitting in the holding cell for hours with nothing to do but think. Things were getting out of hand, and sitting there, I realized I couldn't keep going head up with cats all the time just about my respect. I kept hearing all these guys talking about *you're changing*, and I'd gotten so caught up in trying to keep it real with them when I really needed to be keeping it real with me.

My life *was* changing—that was the whole point. That's why I'd made all the sacrifices I'd made and walked away from the game when I did. Why would I let my pride or something somebody had to say about me hold me back from leveling up? I'd never let somebody try to trick me off the streets so why would I let it happen now? That's not to say I was about to go out like a punk, but I needed to be smart and I needed to evolve. And I needed to embrace the way my life was changing instead of fighting it at every turn.

"Jenkins!"

I looked up and saw an officer walking toward my cell. "Let's go."

I followed him down a long hall and into an interrogation room in the back of the precinct where two detectives were waiting for me. At least that's who I thought they were since they weren't wearing any uniforms. It was a man and a woman, both Latin, and they were standing behind this big-ass table covered in photographs.

"Mr. Jenkins," the woman said. "Have a seat."

As I sat down, I got a better look at all those photos and that's when I realized it was us. And not us, like all the guys I was with that night, but Meech, J-Bo, O-Dog, Bleu, me—everybody. They had shots of us in Cancun, at Magic City, at Compound, at 112, at Crobar, outside the Royal Palm—everywhere.

Then they started asking me all types of questions, and not just about Meech and O-Dog and whoever else had already been caught up. They wanted to know about everybody. And it was clear by their questions that they already knew so much that at a certain point, I was just like, *Man, what* don't *these people know?*

That's when it hit me. They weren't detectives. They were the feds. And as much as you hear about the feds in the streets and people rap about them and all that, the truth is for the most part you never see the feds until it's too late and they're already at your door, or downstairs from your condo asking questions, or in the back of a Miami police precinct with a huge stack of surveillance photos, trying to figure out where you fit in.

I'll admit: for a minute there, I was shook. But once they started asking all those questions, my experience kicked in. I knew I couldn't lie and try to play it like I didn't know certain people or I was never there—they had too much photo evidence for all that—so I just fell back on the best excuse there was. Every time they'd ask me, "Well, how do you know *so-and-so*?"

I'd tell them, "I'm an artist. I know everybody."

"What about *such-and-such*, you know him?"

"Yep," I'd say.

"How?"

"Same thing."

They kept at it for hours, and rather than ask for a lawyer and run the risk of raising any red flags, I just stuck to the script until eventually I drew a line and told them, "Look, if you guys aren't about to charge me with the firearms, then I'm free to go, right?"

By the time I finally got back to where I was staying, I couldn't stop thinking about everything I'd been doing wrong. I'd been so busy trying to stay cool with everybody that I wasn't doing what was right for me. All of that had to end, immediately. And if that meant more static because I had to cut some people off, then so be it. At least if something did happen, I'd know I went out standing up for me.

■ ■ ■

It's one thing to make a decision like that; it's another to live through it. I lost weight from the stress. I lost friends. I even lost the support of the label, for real. There was a long stretch there where it felt like nobody up at Def Jam wanted to answer my calls, and the only person who even bothered to reach out to me was Jay-Z. I'll never forget it. One day he hit me up and asked me if I wanted to talk and we sat up in his executive suite and he heard me out. I was going through so much, and I'd kept it all bottled up for so long, it was almost like a therapy session. I'm not even sure if he knows just how much that talk meant to me at the time, but it meant a lot.

Then, when the government stepped in and shut down my plan to call my clothing line U.S.D.A.—that's how it ended up being 8732 because it was like the old-school beeper codes you'd use to spell things out on a keypad like 8(U)-7(S)-3(D)-2(A)—and school boards all across the country started banning the Snowman shirts, I really felt like I was getting it from all sides. There I was trying to turn my life around and do the so-called "right" thing for the first time in a long, long time, and I felt like nobody wanted to see that for me.

The streets thought I was changing. The mainstream had painted me as a villain. The fans loved my music and my movement, but the label wouldn't pick up the phone. The government was doing everything it could to stop my shine, and to be honest, I didn't really know what to make of the moves I was making either.

All I knew was that I was mad. I was mad at the cats who'd gotten caught up. I was mad at the feds for getting involved. I was mad at all the cats questioning my loyalty and trying me everywhere I went.

And I was mad at me for putting myself in the position I was in in the first place.

My biggest strengths have always been my clarity of vision and purpose. You can take issue with the choices I made and how I set out to go get it, but that was the path I was on from day one, and whenever I might have strayed or things started to get a little out of hand, I was always able to course correct and get back on track.

After all those indictments came down and all these other things started going on, for the first time since I'd arrived at Fort Stewart for the Youth Challenge Program, I was confused. My vision was cloudy, and I didn't know who to trust or where to turn. Of course, it didn't help that I was drinking like a fish. There were months, years even, where I stayed hydrated by drinking champagne. I'm not saying I was a full-blown alcoholic, but for a minute there, I damn sure was close.

I was so paranoid and I felt so isolated that I just leaned into my vices as a way to cope. Days would go by where I would start sipping tequila at two in the afternoon, knowing full well that I still had a whole day of responsibilities ahead of me that wouldn't end until two or three in the morning, and I'd be drinking the whole time. And then there were nights where I would just drive somewhere and sit, drink, and think. Or really, try not to think, just to be real. Just think about that. I had several mansions and condos and all that, but instead of going home, I'd pull into the parking lot behind one of my favorite restaurants, lean the seat back, and drink until I passed out right there in the car.

Looking back, I don't think I was addicted to the alcohol so much as I was just addicted to doing anything I could to numb my pain and quiet my paranoia. I was addicted to the escape. More than anything, though, I was depressed. I'd thought that once I made it in music and had everything that came with it, everybody would be happy for me, but it wasn't like that at all. Even with millions of fans buying my music and screaming my name, I felt more alone than I'd ever been.

When you come from the streets, you think everybody's real until they show you they're not. I'm telling you, I had a lot of people by my side that I thought were solid, and then when it was time to show and prove, come to find out they weren't that at all. And I was devastated by that for real, straight up, because once I saw it for what it was, I didn't know where to turn. I couldn't really talk to anybody in the music industry about it because nobody in the industry was really my peer, not when it came to what I was going through. I'll repeat, in big, bold letters: **Nobody in my era came from where I came from and did what I did in the music industry. Nobody.**

I was in the streets for real, and I came up standing side by side with real, high-level gangsters, mobsters, and killers. Then after Meech and them got locked up, everything turned on a dime. Suddenly, it seemed like everybody who'd been with me was against me, and it got to the point where I felt like I didn't even want to deal with it anymore. I'd get on a flight and the whole time we were in the air, I'd think things might be better for me if the plane would just fall right out of the sky. I never stared down the barrel of my own gun or anything like that, but there were plenty of moments during that stretch where I felt like I was really ready to die.

■ ■ ■

Back in Miami, they ended up charging me with two counts of carrying a concealed firearm without a permit, which never made any sense. I lawyered up and told the police straight up, "If you pull any of my fingerprints off either of those guns, you can lock me up. Otherwise, you can kiss my ass."

Of course, they couldn't do that and a couple of months later, they were forced to drop the charges. Meanwhile the BMF indictments kept coming down. On June 15, 2006, three months after that night in Miami, the DEA swept up sixteen more people including J-Bo and Jacob the Jeweler, and I just knew they were coming for me next.

The whole time I was working on my second album for Def Jam, I'd be having conversations with Shake and Jay-Z about my music one minute, and then I'd be on the phone with somebody's family the next, trying to offer them some kind of comfort or advice. The studio became my sanctuary. I was depressed, stressed, paranoid, and alone, but at least I had my music. That was the one thing that kept me sane. So instead of taking my foot off the gas and celebrating the success of *Thug Motivation* and "Soul Survivor," I stayed in the studio and stayed on my grind.

■ ■ ■

The Inspiration came out on December 12, 2006, and sold over 350,000 copies in its first week of release, twice as many as *Thug Motivation*. I doubled up, just like back on Poplar Street. Matter of fact, *The Inspiration* sold so many copies in that first week that it debuted at number one overall. That was big. A lot of artists struggle with the sophomore slump, but *The Inspiration* showed the whole industry that I was a career artist and not just a flash in the pan.

Looking back, though, I'll be the first to admit that with that album, I tried to whip it up and put it out on the streets while it was still wet. I've always had a big sound, but with *The Inspiration*, I went for an even bigger sound. I tried to take that nine and make it an eighteen, ya dig? And a lot of that came from Shake.

While we were working on that album, he kept bringing me all these monster beats by big-name producers like Cool & Dre, the Runners, and Timbaland. He was challenging me to step up to the plate, and I'm never one to back down from a challenge just like I'm never going to tell myself that I'm not capable of making a major move. So when Shake said he wanted to take Lil Will off the hook of "Go Getta" and have R. Kelly get on there instead, I was with it. Lil Will was my guy, but R. Kelly was *R. Kelly*.

The Inspiration weighed more so it sold more. It happens in the streets all the time. And I can't say it was a mistake because it worked. "I Luv It" and "Go Getta" were both top-20 hits, and when I go back and listen to that album, it still sounds *big*. But the fans let me know that the next time they came to see me, they wanted that straight drop I'd served them that first time around. I can't blame them either. *Thug Motivation* was packed with anthems and made for a time when everybody was getting money. *The Inspiration* was a bigger album made with a smaller audience in mind.

I was speaking directly to the people I knew who were still in the streets and still getting money despite everything. I wanted it to be almost like a pep talk to remind them to keep their head up and keep going because there was a light at the end of the tunnel and a better life was possible. With *The Inspiration*, I was shining that light and waving people on. Knowing what I still had to go through, I can see now how I wasn't just giving everybody else a pep talk. I was trying to do the same thing for me. If you can't inspire yourself, how can you inspire anyone else?

CHAPTER NINETEEN

W.W.J.D.?

Things didn't start to feel like they were really leveling out until sometime in late 2007, but once they did, I went on a hell of a run.

First, Kanye West called. Actually, I called him first. I'd hit him up when I was working on *The Inspiration* to see if he could jump on a song I was putting together called "I Got Money." Well, he did, but when he sent it back to me, he hadn't just put a verse on there—he'd given it the Kanye touch and added all these sound effects and choir and all types of things. When I heard it, I hit him back like, "Yo, my man, I can't rock with this. It's not even the same song!"

But Kanye wasn't tripping. He was just like, "Don't worry about it. It's all good."

I used the original—the one before Kanye got his hands on it—for *The Inspiration*, and then about six months later, I was in LA when Kanye called and asked me to come by the studio. When I pulled up, he was like, "Yo, you know that song you sent me? Check this out."

Imagine my surprise when the song he played for me was basically the same Kanye'd out version of "I Got Money," but now instead of one verse from him, one from me, and one from Tip, it's all Kanye.

And of course Kanye being Kanye, he's looking at me all hyped up like, "That shit's fire, right?"

What was I supposed to say? I mean, it was my song—like that's my song!—but now it wasn't anything like my song. He hadn't even kept my verse. So I just told him what I thought of what he had, like, "Yeah, it's dope." And it was.

He was like, "Hell yeah, it's dope! But, yo, can I keep your ad libs on it?"

Man, I wasn't prepared for that. But I told him he could and after seeing the reaction his version of the song got, I knew Kanye was a genius. He called it "Can't Tell Me Nothing"—I'm guessing you know that one—and what Kanye understood that I didn't even fully get at the time was that the ad libs I was always throwing on my songs and in my verses were like an instrument on their own. So instead of using them to highlight my verse like I'd done on the original version, he used them to heighten the emotion of the production overall and almost bait the audience into sitting on the edge of their seats for the whole song, just waiting for my verse.

At least I know that's the effect it had on me. Even after hearing what he'd played for me in LA, the first time I heard "Can't Tell Me Nothing" on the radio, I heard my ad libs come on and I got hype waiting on my verse like, *Oh, shit, here we go!* Hilarious, right?

But like I said, that's Kanye's genius, and it was dope to be a part of that song even without a verse. Working on that record—or I guess those two records—really solidified our relationship, and when I connected Kanye with Atlanta legend DJ Toomp, who'd produced the original version of the song, they ended up locking in for a lot of Kanye's *Graduation* album, and I know they both appreciated that.

After "Can't Tell Me Nothing," I ended up jumping on a whole bunch of remixes just to get my name back up and basically remind everybody who the fuck I am. That's when I did Shawty Lo's "Dey Know," Rocko's "Umma Do Me," and The-Dream's "I Luv Your Girl." Then I popped up on Mariah Carey's $E=MC^2$ album, which was like a bucket list music moment for me on a bucket list I never even knew I had. Then I talked my way onto a song with Usher after hearing it in the studio one night in early 2008 and that record ended up being a certified smash.

I don't even know if that song was supposed to be a single or what, but the producer was this cat Polow Da Don, and he ended up leaking it when it was done and it pretty much shot straight to the top of the charts. The song was Usher's "Love in This Club." It spent five weeks at the top of the *Billboard* Hot 100, and it's still the biggest record I've ever been a part of to this day. Love Polow for that.

Then I kickstarted the campaign for my third Def Jam album with "Put On," a song I'd put together with a Memphis producer I'd gotten cool with named Drumma Boy and by calling in a favor with Kanye West. I'd thought it might be tough to get Kanye on the line because he'd pretty much been off the grid and lying low mourning the unexpected death of his mom, which was understandable, of course, but when he picked up and I explained that *put on* was sort of Memphis-slash-Atlanta slang for doing it up big, he was like, "Yo, it's all good. I got you."

Twenty minutes after I sent him the beat, he hit me back and just started rapping on the phone like, "I feel like there's still niggas that owe me checks! I feel like there's still bitches that owe me sex!"

"Yo, yo, yo!" I said, jumping in. "Quit rapping! Just go record it! I need that! C'mon!"

As soon as he had it down, he sent it back to me and cc'd L.A. Reid. I hadn't even had a chance to check it out when L.A. hit me up talking about, "When can we put this out? This is the *one!*"

"Put On" dropped right before Memorial Day weekend 2008, and everything was going according to plan. And then Ralphie Simms took the stand as a government witness in the BMF trial and tried to take my whole life away.

■ ■ ■

When it was all said and done, over 150 people were indicted nationwide in the DEA's BMF case, and a lot of those people ended up doing some serious time. J-Bo got fifteen years after pleading guilty to cocaine trafficking and money laundering. Meech eventually pled guilty to money laundering and running a continuing criminal enterprise. Even Jacob the Jeweler got caught up for making false statements to the feds.

Heading into the summer of 2008, I knew I was in a delicate situation and still living on a knife's edge. Then Ralphie Simms said my name in open court.

He was testifying in the case against Fleming "Ill" Daniels, and according to Ralphie, in the fall of 2004, he set aside several kilos for me to pick up from Space Mountain, which was another one of Meech's secret homes. At first, he just said "Jeezy" but then the district attorney asked him to clarify.

"Young Jeezy, the rapper?"

And you know what this motherfucker said? "Yes."

I'll always have love for Meech, but for somebody in his crew to try to throw me under the bus like that, that's where I drew the line. I only knew one way to handle it, and that was to cut ties and distance myself from any- and everything having to do with those three letters.

At the same time I was spiraling out of control. Less than a week after he testified, the cops lit me up late one night when I was riding down I-85 and pulled me over for reckless driving and driving without a license plate. They found an open container in the car and when I failed the sobriety test, they arrested me for DUI.

My third Def Jam album was on deck, but it felt like my life was falling apart. It got to where it felt like everyone around me who'd said they'd love me for life had been spinning a lie. Even Coach. As time went on, it started to feel like we didn't have the same vision and we really weren't seeing eye to eye.

Right or wrong, in a lot of those situations, I blamed myself, but instead of trying to unpack all of those emotions, I bottled it all up and tried to drown the pain. I remember being online one day and stumbling across some photo of me at some event and being stunned by how bad I looked. I was 265 pounds and wildly overweight. My skin looked terrible. My eyes were both yellow and bloodshot.

I couldn't believe I'd let myself go like that. There I was, always talking all that motivation talk trying to inspire everybody who ever listened to me to improve their lives and I wasn't even taking care of my own. *Let's get it* doesn't work if the *let's* doesn't include me.

I buckled down.

I started learning about nutrition and taking it seriously. I cut back on my drinking, I stopped going out, and I locked myself in the studio for two months. Just like I'd done with *Trap or Die* and *Thug Motivation*, I put everything I was feeling into my music. That was my therapy.

Eventually, I called up one of my guys, and when I played him the music I'd been working on, he just looked at me and said, "That's it right there. You're done."

■ ■ ■

The Recession came out on September 2, 2008, and debuted at the top of the *Billboard* charts with 260,000 copies sold in the first week, giving me back-to-back number ones. The response was incredible. Right away, the fans, the critics, and the culture all let me know that *The Recession* was a classic.

Turns out I wasn't the only one who'd been going through it. The whole country was hurting. The whole world, really. The global economy was a mess and people everywhere were losing their jobs, their homes, and their life savings. There were wars going on in Iraq and Afghanistan, a presidential election on deck—Barack Obama vs. John McCain—and suddenly that word—*recession*—was on everybody's lips. My album was right on time.

The same way *Tha Streets Iz Watchin*, *Trap or Die*, and *Thug Motivation* ended up being the soundtrack to that whole era in Atlanta, *The Recession* was the music of the moment. "Put On" was the anthem that summer—the rest of that year, really—and it was another top-20 hit. And then "My President" went on to become the unofficial theme song of the Obama campaign.

I'd recorded that record when Obama and Hillary Clinton were still battling it out in the primary, and we leaked it on August 20, just days before the Democratic National Convention. Even though a lot of people looked at me crazy when it first came out—like, *Yo, Jeezy's talking politics now? What the fuck?*—with Obama on the ticket and so much at stake, I felt like I had to get involved.

And after I named the album *The Recession* months before the government even officially declared we were in a recession and over the objections of the people up at Def Jam—for real, you should have heard their reaction when I told them the name, like, "*The Recession*? Nobody even knows what the fuck that is!"—*and* I had "My President" out months before the inauguration, I didn't just look like a genius, I looked like a prophet.

I'll never forget riding down Peachtree the night Obama won. I was in my Jeezy blue Lamborghini with the doors up, blasting "My

President" and people were out in traffic hollering at me like, "We did it, Jeezy! We won!"

America had been around for something like 230 years and finally our president—my president—was Black. For the first time in a long, long time, I started to have a little hope.

Today was a good day, hope I have me a great night
I don't know what you fishin' for, but catch you a great
    white
Me, I seen great white, heavy as killer whales
I cannot believe this, who knew it came in bales?
Who knew it came with jail? Who knew it came with prison?
Just 'cause you got opinions, that make you a politician?
Bush robbed all of us, what that make him? A criminal
He cheated in Florida, what that make him, a Seminole?
I say and I quote, we need a miracle
And I say a miracle 'cause this shit is hysterical
On my nephews and nieces, I will email Jesus
Tell him to forward to Moses and cc Allah
I'm just a sole survivor, does that make me a convict?
"Be all you can be," now don't that sound like some dumb
    shit?
When we're dying for crude oil black as my nigga Bu
It's really a desert storm, that's word to my nigga Clue
Catch me in Las Vegas, AR, Arizona
Rep for them real niggas, I'm winning in California
Winning in Tennessee, hands down Atlanta
Landslide Alabama on my way to Savannah

My president is Black, my Lambo's blue
And I'll be goddamned if my rims ain't, too

Mama ain't at home, daddy's still in jail
Tryna make a play, anybody seen the scale?

■ ■ ■

I can honestly say that it wasn't until after *The Recession* came out that I finally felt like a star. I'd spent the summer of 2008 getting my mind and my body right. I'd dropped a bunch of weight and started eating right, drinking plenty of water, and working out. And I could see the results. If you look at any photos of me from back then, even *The Recession* album cover, my eyes are clear, and I had a six-pack underneath my vest.

Just the simple act of taking better care of myself day to day made a world of difference. Instead of feeling like the weight of the world was on my shoulders when I woke up, with my head and body heavy from going so hard the night before, I felt refreshed and light, focused and ready to seize the day. Eating and drinking right didn't solve all my problems—not at all—but it put me in a better place and a better mind state so I felt more fully resourced and prepared to face those problems with clarity.

I'd just had to get back to listening to my own advice. For years, I'd always tell people whenever you feel stuck, just take one simple step in any direction. It doesn't matter, just get moving; and then once you start moving, just keep taking those steps and keep going. You'll be amazed at how far you can go.

I got new management and landed deals with brands like Belvedere and Boost Mobile for national campaigns. I did an Adidas collaboration and got more active in the community, helping people out through my Street Dreamz Foundation and doing things like voter registration drives. I even registered to vote—and voted—myself.

I also started really building my empire. I invested in real estate all over Atlanta and California. I became a partner in Avión Tequila, got hands-on with our marketing, and did very well when we sold to Pernod Ricard in 2018. I invested in American Cut Steakhouse, and got equity stakes in a water company, Defiance Fuel, and Naud Spirits. I started my own management company, Agency 99, and eventually even became a Def Jam executive myself.

After *The Recession*, I finally felt free. I don't know if it was because Ralphie Simms was a cooperating witness so his testimony didn't stand up or the feds really didn't have anything solid to pin on me or what, but for whatever reason, when Operation Motor City was all said and done, I was never charged. I wish I could say the same for everyone else. About a week after *The Recession* came out, Meech and his brother, Terry, were each sentenced to thirty years, and for the most part, that was the end of the case.

I really don't know how I managed to avoid getting caught up. I actually ran into O-Dog not too long ago at a car wash. He'd done his time and come home, but I hadn't seen him in years. We chopped it up a little bit and then we both went our separate ways, and all I could think about as I was driving home was just how different our paths had been. We'd both been right there together in the clubs, throwing money, acting a fool, living the life, and having the time of our lives. But at a certain point, I went right and threw myself into my music and he went the other way. It's crazy how God works. He used to always laugh at me for trying to be a rapper.

■ ■ ■

One Sunday not too long after *The Recession* came out, I was sitting on the front porch of the four-bedroom house I'd bought my mom in

South Georgia, on plenty of land, when Kanye called and asked if I could get on a plane.

I was like, "Sure, no problem. What for?"

"I just want you to come."

I touched down in Hawaii the very next day, and Kanye being Kanye, when I hit him up to let him know I was there, he didn't answer the phone. I spent the whole day on the beach like, *Fuck it. I guess I'll make the best of it.* And honestly, that was a great day. I like spending time alone. It gives me the time to get into my thoughts.

It had been over twenty years since I'd lived on base at K-Bay, and as I sat down to dinner with the sun setting over that picture-perfect ocean view, all these memories of my life on base came flooding back. I imagined there was probably some kid from Georgia over there at that exact moment, feeling just like I'd felt, a fish out of water, too country for the locals and so far away from home. If I could, I'd tell him to enjoy the moment and not sweat the small stuff. Being able to travel is a gift that a lot of people never get, especially people coming from where we're from, and it will expand your horizons if you let it. The road hadn't been easy, but I know it had expanded mine.

"Yo, my bad," Kanye said, when he hit me the next day. He was working out of Avex Honolulu Studios, right on the coast, and he asked me to come through. When I pulled up on him that night, I had no idea what to expect.

Kanye was in the middle of a two-month break from the Glow in the Dark Tour and he'd been in Hawaii working for weeks. I knew he had a couple of projects on his plate—Jay's *Blueprint 3* and his own album, which he'd been teasing for months. And of course, Kanye being Kanye, for all I knew he might be working on some whole other shit.

When I walked in, the first thing I saw was this big-ass whiteboard with a list of what I figured must be a whole bunch of song titles on one side and then right there at the top of the board in big, bold handwritten letters: WHAT WOULD JEEZY DO?

I laughed. "Man, *What would Jeezy do?* What's that?"

'Ye launched into an explanation, and again, Kanye being Kanye, he was hype.

"Yo, so you know how cats be having those bumper stickers, right? Like, *What would Jesus do?* Well, we decided to switch it up, and the whole time we've been working on this album, that's what we keep asking. Like, every time I write a chorus or some type of hook, I'll ask everyone in the room, like, *All right, yeah, but what would Jeezy do?* Like, what would you say on the record if you were here?"

I laughed again. "Is that right?"

He was like, "Hell yeah! That's why I needed you out here, bro. I need to get your opinion on these songs!"

He was dead serious, too, and for the next few days, I sat out there in the studio with them and we went through all the songs he'd been working on. Whenever I'd start bobbing my head to something, somebody would go up to that board and make a mark. Eventually there were all these song titles that had marks next to them and all of these others that didn't, and I guess he ended up factoring all of that feedback in when it came time to put together *808s & Heartbreak* later on.

The whole process reminded me of how it would go whenever I'd play my songs for Hov. We'd talk about the records here and there, but for the most part I'd just watch his reactions and if I could tell he was feeling something, I'd make a mental note like, *That's the one.*

I can't front, though, it definitely tripped me out to find myself playing that position for Kanye West. It made me think of a line I'd had on "U.S.D.A., Pt. 2" from *Trap or Die*:

They say I can't rap, I hear a lot of things
Still I bounce on the track like a trampoline . . .

I'd written that line after all those late nights at Patchwerk with O-Dog and all of them pulling up on me talking shit, and all those sessions in Shawty's basement with one of his homegirls constantly coming down there, talking about how we needed to stop wasting our time because the music shit would never work.

And yet there I was, out in Hawaii, in a multimillion-dollar studio a stone's throw from K-Bay with Kanye West, a straight-up musical genius, and when he's looking for feedback on his new album, he's looking at me.

I'd come a long, long—*long*—way.

■ ■ ■

A little over a month later, I was in Tallahassee getting ready for a show. It was homecoming week for Florida A&M and I was co-headlining the big concert with Tip after the Morgan State vs. FAMU game. It was going to be a huge show. I was fresh off *The Recession* and Tip had just dropped his sixth album, *Paper Trail*, which went gold right out the gate so you already know Tallahassee was about to turn up.

I'd spent the morning working at a Get Out the Vote phone bank in Atlanta for the Obama campaign, literally calling people up and reading off a list of talking points they'd given me like, "This is Young Jeezy calling on behalf of the Obama campaign . . ."

You can imagine some of the reactions I got. There were a fair number of seniors who didn't really know who I was, but more than a few times, it was fans screaming like, "Mama! Young Jeezy on the phone!"

We'd driven down to Tallahassee that afternoon, and I was sitting on my tour bus going through my pre-show routine when Kink's number popped up on my phone. I could tell something was wrong just by the sound of his voice. Kink's usually a bit of a high-energy dude, but on that call, he was way more subdued. There was a long pause and then he finally told me the news. Shake was gone.

I was like, "Gone? What the fuck you mean, *gone*?"

Kink gathered himself on the other end of the line. "He's gone, man," he said, finally. "They found him this afternoon. He took his own life."

The news damn near knocked me off my feet. My legs started shaking and my hands and lips went cold, and I wanted to scream so loud. I felt like someone had stabbed me in the heart. I thought about grabbing the wheel and ramming the bus into a brick wall, anything to take the pain away. Really, I wanted to do anything to bring him back. But that was never going to happen. Like Kink had said, Shake was gone.

Losing Shake was like nothing I'd ever experienced. Where I come from, people don't take their own lives. I feel like maybe you're seeing a little bit more of it now, but back then, it was like a totally foreign concept. I've lost people to the street life and gang violence, and I've seen it all firsthand. But nothing I'd ever seen, heard, or experienced prepared me for getting that news about Shake. In the Black community, suicide is one of those things we tell ourselves, *That doesn't happen to us.*

I'd just talked to him, too. I could tell he was acting a little different, but I never would have imagined it would have come to that. Not in a million years. He had a young family, and his career was climbing to new heights. He was already certified—the success he'd had with signing me and Rick Ross at Def Jam, not to mention Beyoncé at HitCo and Ciara at Arista, would have made him a legend for life. But in June, he'd stepped into an even bigger role: executive vice president of Def Jam, essentially taking over the label from Jay-Z.

In an industry chock full of fake love, fake conversations, fake promises, and fake friends, with Shake it always felt real. When it came to music, he was like a big brother to me, and one of my few close, trusted friends. And now my guy—the guy who believed in me when no one else did, and who'd basically saved my life by giving me a shot—was in the big chair at Def Jam, and I just knew we were going to do even bigger things. With *The Recession*, we were off to a great start. It still hurts to know that was as far as we would go.

Shake was thirty-four when he died, I was thirty-one, and it's hard not to get caught up in wondering if there were any signs I missed or what I could have done differently or said. I would give anything to go back in time and talk to him in those days that led up to him doing what he did. I wish I could tell him that no matter what was going on, he wasn't alone because I was right there, and the only thing I couldn't protect him from was himself.

If he'd laid it all out for me—whatever was going on—and then asked me, like, "Man, what would you do?" I would have told him what I'm about to tell you. I really believe that we're all only here for two reasons: to love and to learn.

A whole lot of us have to learn how to love ourselves and others—but the rest of the lessons are right there in our own lives, and there's really no getting around it. We're all going to go through our own trials and tribulations, and you can try to run from your problems and drown them in your vices—whether that's drinking or drugs or whatever else—but that's just going to make your problems worse and that lesson you need that much harder to learn.

No one's path is perfect. Most people's paths aren't pretty. But we're all on the path. If you find yourself getting lost and you're in the dark, just remember—you're not alone. There is somebody out there who loves you. Usually, a lot more people than you might think, and if given the opportunity, all of them want to help. There's nothing wrong with asking for help either, so reach out. I know that can be hard, especially when you're at your lowest point, but the most important thing is to stay in the fight and just keep going. That doesn't mean it's going to be easy or that everything is going to work out the way you want it to, but that's the only way you'll learn. And that's why we're all here in the first place.

I miss Shake every day. And to anyone else who might find themselves thinking those thoughts, if you can't find a loved one or a friend to talk to, pick up the phone, call 988, and get the help you need.

Stay up. And keep going.

CHAPTER TWENTY

Evolve or Die

At first, I didn't want to do Verzuz.

Don't get me wrong, the concept was dope—two artists facing off and trading songs in front of an audience to determine who "won"—but when it first really started popping off at the height of the COVID-19 pandemic, I didn't think it was for me. It felt like it was geared more toward the old-school legacy acts. Say what you want: I know what I'm cooking up, and I'm still going strong.

When Larry Jackson over at Apple Music started hitting me up talking about how he thought I should do a Verzuz with Gucci Mane, I had to tell him thanks but no thanks, like, "Bro, this shit is deeper than you think."

Apple Music was in business with Verzuz at the time, and I felt like what Larry was talking about would be good for them. But in the grand scheme of things, I wasn't sure if it would be good for us.

Then Swizz Beatz started calling me. Now, if you don't know the origins of Verzuz, Swizz and Timbaland started it together, and then they went out and sold it to the world. Swizz was in my ear trying to sell me on it, like, "Jeezy, this shit is going to be bigger than life, I'm telling you!"

At the time, the Black Lives Matter movement had just taken hold, and it seemed like every time you got on the internet or turned on the news, all you were seeing were stories of young Black men being killed all over the world, at the hands of the police and otherwise. It made me think maybe Swizz was right after all. Maybe the culture needed me and Radric to share the stage.

Then T.I. went on Instagram Live or something talking about how I didn't want to see him in a Verzuz, and that really caught me off guard. After all these years, Tip and I are sort of like brothers, and we can talk about all sorts of things, and we do, all the time. So when I heard him talking about how "Jeezy don't want this smoke," I felt some type of way because I'd just talked to him, and he'd never said anything like that to me.

But that's Tip. He's always going to speak his mind and ride his own wave, and he knows how to entertain.

I jumped out there and responded to Tip with a video of my own letting him know he didn't want it with Big Sno, and then Larry and Swizz started calling me all over again and for a minute there, that was the play: Jeezy and Tip, Verzuz. Coming soon. It was locked in. We even posted the flyers.

One day in November 2020, I was doing an interview with *The Breakfast Club* promoting the talk show I had on Fox Soul at the time, *Worth a Conversation*, as well as letting the world know that my new album, *The Recession 2*, was coming soon, when Angela Yee and Charlamagne started asking me about Verzuz. Instead of getting into all the back-and-forth negotiations behind the scenes, I decided I'd tell them how I was really feeling at the time.

If I was going to do a Verzuz, it would only be right—for the fans, for the culture, and for us as artists and men—for it to be me and Gucci Mane.

. . .

When I pulled into the Magic City parking lot that night, the air was so thick and there were so many guns out there, it looked like Beirut. He had his people standing next to his Rolls-Royce truck, and of course I had mine already out there, scattered.

We'd actually sat down, just us, at the St. Regis in Buckhead beforehand, and come to an understanding that whatever happened, we weren't going to kill each other in front of the world. Still, nobody knew what to expect once we got on that stage. Even the Verzuz people had started having second thoughts. Swizz hit me up a couple of days before the event like, "Yo, can you believe everybody wants me to cancel?"

I was like, "Really? Well, yeah. I could see that."

When I pulled up, Magic—the guy who owns Magic City—came out to the parking lot and started hollering at everybody like, "Yo, what the hell is going on? Y'all got it looking like a Navy SEALs thing out here! You know I ain't going to let nothing happen to y'all, c'mon!"

Magic is sort of like everybody's uncle because he's known all of us for so long. That was part of my thinking about wanting to do it at Magic City in the first place, especially after Radric signed on. Just out of respect, you don't go to dinner at your uncle's house and just start acting a fool, no matter how heated things get. The way I was looking at it, whatever would happen would happen. But at least if it went left, it would happen outside and not be broadcast live all over the world because that would be a bad look for everyone involved— me, him, Magic, Swizz and Timbaland, Apple Music, Instagram, and the whole Verzuz platform. The city of Atlanta, and the whole culture, really. I was banking on our mutual respect for Magic and Magic City to help us keep our emotions in check.

■ ■ ■

He went in with his people first, and as I sat in the back of my Bentley Mulsanne waiting on my negative COVID test to come back, I collected myself and focused on everything I had going on, everything I had in the works, and everything I came there that night to do.

What you've got to understand is that I know Radric. Like, I know him for real, for real, before all the Gucci Mane shit and all of that. I knew no matter what he'd been talking about in the press about how he'd come home from prison a changed man, he was going to get up there on that stage and try to pull his antics in front of the world, and it was going to be on me to figure out how I was going to react.

Was I going to go back to being *Young* Jeezy, the pistol-toting fool who doesn't give a fuck and ain't got shit to live for, with one foot in and one foot out of the streets, so paranoid he can't sleep, willing to do whatever, whenever, to defend his pride and protect his ego, including fuck up all of the good things he's got going on that are really nothing but God's blessings? Or was I going to put all the work I'd been doing on myself to the test, and not react to whatever he tried to pull?

The way I was looking at it, as much as that night was about us, it wasn't about me. It was about standing up for the culture and creating a moment. Even more than that, though, it was about setting an example for the next generation, like, even when you've been through everything that Radric and I had been through, it doesn't have to end like *that*. We had the chance to change the narrative and do what 'Pac and Big never got the chance to do. It might not save the lives of everybody out there in the middle of some type of beef, but it might save a few.

I just had to keep my cool.

■ ■ ■

Sitting in my Bentley, I thought about all the legendary nights I'd had right there in that room. All the people I'd met—from J-Bo to Tip to Fabolous to literally hundreds, probably thousands more. All the business I'd done, and all the money I'd thrown. Magic City is one of those spots that truly changed my life—in both games.

That night, I was taking it all the way back to the essence with me—custom-made, Exclusive Game Big Sno jersey, black bandana, and a fresh white pair of Air Force 1s. I wanted to remind the world that as much as I'd evolved as an artist and as a man, there were parts of my past and my legacy that you could never erase. I may know a whole lot more these days about how to wear a well-tailored three-piece suit, where to vacation in the South of France, and how to go into a boardroom full of executives and close a deal anywhere in the world, but I'm still that same guy who came in the game fresh off the block, put the streets on my back, and made history with no lies and no gimmicks, for real.

In real life, I always thought it was *la costa nostra*, this thing of ours, but as social media has taken over the world, I've realized that people will do and say anything to try to assassinate your character, especially when they resent your success. I've still got an ear to the street, and of course I hear the interviews. Seems to me like it's just a whole lot of talking, and the way I was raised, that ain't what made men do. All I know is that everything I ever did, I did it with honor, integrity, dignity, and grace. Just know: if you're winning, they're going to hate; if you're losing, they're going to laugh; and if it's gotta be you or them, it's always going to be you.

I thought back on what it felt like that first night I'd pulled up when "Over Here" was going off. The record hadn't worked at first, but DJ Nando kept giving it a shot until it broke. And it wasn't just

"Over Here" either. Nando broke all my songs for years. As the DJ for Magic City Mondays, he made it to where whenever I walked in, they'd play my music for four hours straight, with everybody in there rapping along, word for word. Love Nando for that, and over the years we developed a real relationship, and he became one of my good friends.

I remembered what he always used to say to me whenever something would pop off, and for a while there, things were always popping off. He'd be like, "Jeezy, you're bigger than all this shit, bro. You can't let these cats trick you off the street, because if they trick you, you're done."

In 2013, somebody caught Nando coming home from the club and shot and killed him right in his front yard. That was another one of those losses that really stayed with me, and that night at Verzuz I could feel his presence as soon as I stepped into the club. And I could hear his voice, too, like, "They're going to try to trick you, dog. This is it. Right here, tonight."

I had to ask myself, in the heat of the moment, which side of me would I show?

■ ■ ■

The first thing I noticed when I walked in was that it was a light room. There were maybe about fifty people there. DJ Drama was in there, and Rick Ross was, too. And it seemed like some of the people were choosing sides. I saw Larry Jackson was sort of standing over on Radric's side, and there were a couple people on mine, and when I peeped that, I was like, *Well, okay.*

We took our seats on the two thrones they had set up for us on opposite sides of the stage, and then boom, right out the gate he does

"Round 1 (Gucci vs. Jeezy)," which is the same song he put out when I was laid up recovering from throat surgery.

All of a sudden, I was reliving all that trauma and all those old memories, and I can't front, watching him perform that record right there in front of my face had me heated, but I kept telling myself, "Man, whatever happens, don't lose *you*. If you let this man antagonize you to the point where you do something out of character, that's not you taking control of the situation; that's him controlling you."

As heated as I was, I played it cool and stuck to my plan, and as we got into the records, I just felt like, *Man, there's no way anything he's ever done is standing up to my catalog.* He played his next song, and I did "Trap or Die." He played his next record, and I did "Standing Ovation." And we just kept going like that.

He'd play his little songs, and I'd play my anthems. After a while, I started to notice his team scrambling trying to figure out what to play next, but I wasn't stressing because there aren't a whole lot of artists out there who can really see me record for record. I've got too many classics, for real.

Then he tried to take a little jab at me like, "Man, quit playing all those old-ass songs." He looked at me and smiled, and just to keep it real, that's when I knew he knew that he was fucked because I still had a full clip of hits left. Then he did "Truth."

Everybody on my team started screaming, "'Stay Strapped!' Get him! Play 'Stay Strapped!'"

If I'm honest, if I had played "Stay Strapped" it would have been lights out. At the same time, I knew that was the defining moment of the whole night. That was the moment of truth. Was I going to evolve or die?

My grandmother used to always tell me that I was a natural born leader, and she was absolutely right. The funny thing is, the very same things she thought would destroy me—the streets and the game—actually gave me a foundation to stand on. Even though she never lived to see it, I know she's proud of me. And just like them nines and them O's, I had to take all my trials and tribulations and bag them all up. ADVERSITY FOR $ALE.

ACKNOWLEDGMENTS

JEEZY would like to thank the streets, God, his family, his day ones, and every DJ who ever played his records, every exec and everybody who ever believed in his vision and inspired him to keep going. To anybody out there who's going through trials and trills, just know that if you do what's easy, life will be hard, and if you do what's hard, life will be easy. You gotta believe.

■ ■ ■

BENJAMIN MEADOWS-INGRAM would like to thank Jeezy for the years of trust, candor, hospitality, and inspiration. It's been an honor and a privilege. Here's to more greatness to come. Thanks to Solo for facilitating everything, and Dave, Azee, Travis, and the rest of the team for all of the help along the way. Thanks to Marcie Cleary, truly the best lawyer in the game, and my agent, Anthony Mattero, who's shown himself to be a real standup guy in a game where that's not a given. Thanks to the lovely Jan Miller and Ali Kominsky at Dupree Miller for all of the support throughout this process. You've been a dream to work with and this book doesn't happen without you. Respect. To the HarperCollins Leadership team—thank you for believing in this project and for all of your patience and hard work in bringing it home. Thank you to DJ Drama for your time and insight through the years on all things and the good people at

Patchwerk for the open door. Thanks to Frazier Tharpe for getting in the trenches with me, and Spencer Gaffney for the invaluable bird's eye view. Thanks to Damien Lemon, Rondell Conway, Noah Callahan-Bever, Toshitaka Kondo, Brendan Frederick, Chris Yuscavage, Damien Scott, Rob Kenner, Donnie Kwak, Mimi Valdéz, Shani Parish, Jon Caramanica, Sean Fennessey, and the whole VIBE and Mass Appeal extended fams for the entire ride. Thanks to Gabe Tesoriero, Peter Kadin, and Sarah Cunningham for always making things happen. To Danyel Smith and Elliott Wilson, I'm forever grateful for the love, friendship, and more. To the cities and people of Memphis and Atlanta—thank you. Salute to David Ka, Diwang Valdez, and Sebastian Urrea, and the whole Motion Family massive. And my eternal love and gratitude to Ileana, who's always believed.

SONG CREDITS

"OVER HERE"

"AIR FORCES"

"TRAP OR DIE"

"INTRO TO TRAP OR DIE"

"BOTTOM OF THE MAP"

"GET YA MIND RIGHT"
© 2005 EMI April Music Inc., EMI Blackwood Music Inc., Shawty Redd Songs, & Young Jeezy Music Inc.
All rights administered by Sony Music Publishing (US) LLC, 424 Church Street, Suite 1200, Nashville, TN 37219. All rights reserved. Used by permission.

"MY PRESIDENT"
Words and Music by Justin Keith Henderson, Nasir Jones, Christopher John Whitacre, (Jay W. Jenkins)
© Song Of Universal, Inc. on behalf of itself, Henderworks Publishing Co. and Nappypub Music, Universal Music - Z Songs on behalf of itself and Sun Shining, Inc., Universal Music Corp. on behalf of itself, Nappy Boy Publishing and West Coast Livin Publishing (ASCAP, BMI)

Everybody was hype
Pull up at my friend

ABOUT THE AUTHOR

JAY "JEEZY" JENKINS is a born hustler turned urban philosopher, turned entrepreneur. This is his first book.

p 77-78 switching to music
r way out r

p. 80 Ho learned how "not" to do it

p 81 cousins/family. Seeing through the eyes
of an adult, and that cousins weren't who
he thought

p 87 starting to rap, failing for years, but consistently
practicing

p 89. Shanty Red → experience hanging a/him and
watching and learning was like grad school.

p 92 All the constant stress, fear, any moment could
be his last. And all after their first album
failed. so a lot of doubt. 24 yrs old

p 95-96. Never stole (not big) except for payback on his
cousin who stole his 250k.
Also, introd God a lot for first time—

move
p 122 Just more when you're stuck or overwhelmed
121 take a concrete step in the direction
you're trying to move.

p. 122 Every artist needs the smart ear who
will give them honest feedback.

p 124 It Atlanta your music doesn't go anywhere
if out the strip clubs behind you. Wow. who knew

p 136 once eating well, taking next step of
integrity — right action in right direction
get moving.